Simeon's Story

An Eyewitness Account of the Kidnapping of Emmett Till

SIMEON WRIGHT

WITH HERB BOYD

Lawrence Hill Books

Chicago

The Library of Congress has cataloged the hardcover edition as follows:
Wright, Simeon, 1942–
  Simeon's story : an eyewitness account of the kidnapping of Emmett Till / Simeon
Wright ; with Herb Boyd. — 1st ed.
    p. cm.
  Includes index.
  ISBN 978-1-55652-783-8
  1. Till, Emmett, 1941–1955—Juvenile literature. 2. Mississippi—Race relations—
Juvenile literature. 3. Lynching—Mississippi—History—20th century—Juvenile
literature. 4. African Americans—Crimes against—Mississippi—History—20th
century—Juvenile literature. 5. African American teenage boys—Mississippi—
Biography—Juvenile literature. 6. Racism—Mississippi—History—20th century—
Juvenile literature. 7. Trials (Murder)—Mississippi—Juvenile literature. I. Boyd,
Herb, 1938– II. Title.
  E185.93.M6W83 2010
  305.8009762—dc22

                                    2009033631

Cover design: Joan Sommers Design
Front cover photos, clockwise from top: Site of Emmett Till's kidnapping,
photo © Ed Clark/Time Life Pictures/Getty Images; Emmett Till, author's
collection; Store belonging to murderer Roy Bryant, photo © Ed Clark/Time Life
Pictures/Getty Images; Simeon Wright, author's collection; Picking cotton,
photo by Marion Post Wolcott, Library of Congress, LC-USF33-030629-M3.
Interior design: Jonathan Hahn
All interior images from the author's collection.

Copyright © 2010 by Simeon Wright and Herb Boyd
All rights reserved
First hardcover edition published 2010
First paperback edition published 2011
Published by Lawrence Hill Books
An imprint of Chicago Review Press, Incorporated
814 North Franklin Street
Chicago, Illinois 60610
ISBN 978-1-56976-819-8
Printed in the United States of America
5 4 3 2 1

To my dad, Moses Wright.
This black man facing racism alone uttered
these words when pressured not to take part
in the trial of Emmett Till's murderers:
"I know one thing—I know I am going to testify.
Whether I'll live, I don't know."

Contents

Foreword by Herb Boyd   ix

Acknowledgments   xv

1

Life in Mississippi   1

2

My Family   15

3

At Home with Mom and Dad   25

4

The Abduction   41

5

The Trial   67

6

Fear and Flight   81

7

In Argo   91

8

Reopening the Case and Exhuming the Body   105

9

Bobo on My Mind   115

Epilogue: The Till Bill   123
Appendix: Lies, Myths, and Distortions   129
Index   139

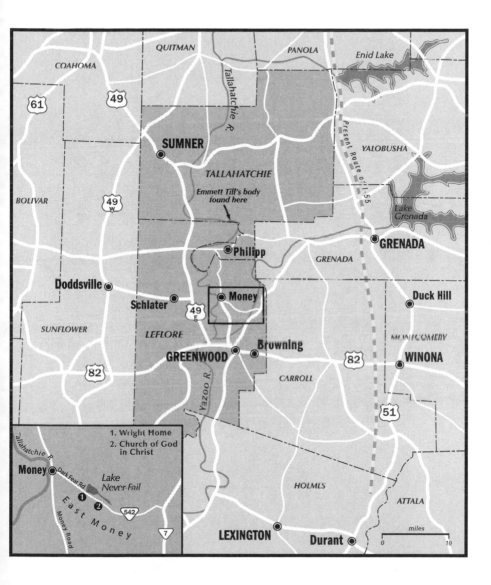

COAHOMA

QUITMAN

PANOLA

Enid Lake

61

49

SUMNER

YALOBUSHA

Tallahatchie R.

TALLAHATCHIE

Present Route 0f I-55

BOLIVAR

49
W

Emmett Till's body
found here

Lake
Grenada

GRENADA

Philipp

GRENADA

Doddsville

Money

Duck Hill

Schlater

49
E

SUNFLOWER

LEFLORE

MONTGOMERY

82

GREENWOOD

Browning

WINONA

Yazoo R.

CARROLL

82

51

1. Wright Home
2. Church of God
in Christ

Tallahatchie R.

Money

Dark Fear Rd

Lake
Never-Fail

HOLMLS

ATTALA

1

2

East Money

542

miles

Money Road

7

LEXINGTON

Durant

0   10

Foreword

by Herb Boyd

I FIRST MET SIMEON WRIGHT IN 2002, when filmmaker Keith Beauchamp was traveling around the country previewing his documentary *The Untold Story of Emmett Louis Till*. At each place in the New York area where the film was screened—New York University, the United Nations, and the Film Forum—Simeon, and sometimes his wife, Annie, helped Keith promote his film about the tragic death of Simeon's cousin.

During one of those visits, Simeon and I talked extensively about the incident and how it had affected him over the years, and especially now that the film was getting such good notices. Simeon confessed to me that without Keith's persistence he never would have been part of the project, since he holds bitter memories about other attempts to capture his cousin's story.

So many lies, distortions, and inaccuracies about Till's death had accumulated over the years that Simeon had become increasingly upset and had begged off when writers, reporters, and filmmakers tried to involve him in recounting what had happened that fateful morning years ago. Even I was beginning to sense that I was annoying him with my questions during my interviews with him after the screenings, but I was mistaken—he assured me that Keith had done a good job and he felt a bit more willing to talk about the murder and the cousin he called Bobo.

"What about telling your own version of what happened and not be part of somebody else's project?" I asked him.

"Well, I'll have to think about it," he said, and his old reluctance to reveal his innermost feelings crept into our conversation.

Several weeks, if not months, went by, and I hadn't heard from Simeon, when Keith said that he wanted to speak to me. They had been together at one of the events in Mississippi in honor of Till when Simeon expressed a desire to talk to me. I called him immediately, and he said—thanks to his wife's badgering—he was ready to write his autobiography. Annie, my coconspirator, had quietly talked to me about a possible book on Simeon's life, but I had seen those moments as merely fun and games between us, nothing resembling a secret attempt to get him to commit. Anyway, her cajoling and pleading finally pushed Simeon to the point where he was ready to put his memories down on paper. It was time to set the record straight, he said.

When we finally got down to business, I had just completed a book on the civil rights movement with Ossie Davis and Ruby Dee, and so the Emmett Till case was fresh on my mind again. I was a teenager when Till was brutally murdered in Mississippi, only two years older than he was, and it was hard for me even to look at his battered face that appeared in photos circulated by my mother's friends and neighbors. All I can remember of those days is that my mother seemed to be grateful that she had found the means and wherewithal to spirit my brother and me out of the South.

Not having daily contact with the white world, my friends and I in the ghettos of Detroit were stunned to learn that Till had been killed for merely whistling at a white woman. It gave us pause, but we felt secure, since we were assured that something like that could never happen in the North, and especially not in Detroit.

Working with Simeon and listening to him recall his childhood in Mississippi and his youth near Chicago reminded me of my early years. I was born in Birmingham, Alabama, but spent the first years of my life outside Tuskegee in a tiny enclave called Cotton Valley. Simeon left the South when he was twelve; my mother got us out of Dixie when I was four. So his memories of the South are much sharper than any I can conjure.

This is Simeon's story, and it is one I believe he could have written without me. But I like to think that my coaxing, goading, and pushing him deeper into his memories played at least a small part in getting the book completed. As many of us know, memory is not the most reliable of our faculties. Part of my responsibility was to help him pinpoint certain moments and to put them in historical and political context. I was aware of Simeon's concern that the book be his and not the ruminations of a ghostwriter seeking a way to tell his own story. Occasionally I have imposed my ideas on Simeon, but only in those instances where a little more backstory, statistics, or additional research enriches a passage. Otherwise, this is Simeon's story, his narrative, and I think he's done a marvelous job exhuming thoughts and events that must have been painful to relive. Sure he had talked about those episodes, both publicly and privately, but now he had to put things down on paper, which is never an easy task.

Even so, Simeon is a storyteller of the highest order, and it has been a pleasure journeying with him back over the years and, in a literary manner, meeting those friends and relatives whom I now count among my extended family. I came to really know Bobo and the world that shaped him and Simeon. To a great extent that world hasn't changed that much, though I leave that judgment to you after you've read Simeon's story.

Simeon saw his cousin taken from his family, never to return. His story should have a special resonance for readers both young and old. As he looks back on this tragic moment in his childhood, we hope that you can identify with the trauma he experienced and understand why what happened years ago in Mississippi is still an important chapter in our nation's history.

Acknowledgments

THANKS TO MY WIFE, who suggested that I write a book about Emmett to set the record straight about his kidnapping and murder. She constantly reminded me about the importance of having an eyewitness account of what happened on the fateful nights of August 24 and 28, 1955. I am thankful for her persistence and tenacity. Without her encouragement I probably would be still procrastinating. Annie, thank you for your love and support.

Thanks to Keith Beauchamp, a young filmmaker who insisted that it was essential I tell the story of Emmett Till for the sake of the truth. He said that in his research of the case he found many inaccuracies. But what amazed him is what he did not find. Those he talked to had never sat down and talked with those who were involved in the story—the eyewitnesses. He did not find any writings based on testimony from the primary sources. His constant word to me was, "Mr. Wright, only you can tell what happened at the store and what happened in the bedroom. Secondary sources cannot tell your story." He pointed out to me that people are not interested in information about Emmett; they want the *truth* about Emmett. Keith said, "You have the truth; no one can tell it like you can tell it." Thanks, Keith, for saying to me, "You must write the book about Emmett."

Thanks to Sojourn to the Past, a living black history class of high school juniors and seniors who were moved by the Till story. Their passion and hunger for the truth about Emmett Till moved me to promise them that I would write this book. These children literally pulled the story out of me. Sojourn, starting with the classes of 2006–2009, thank you for your love and encouragement. You have been a great inspiration to me.

Lastly, thanks to my nephew Wheeler Parker Jr. Wheeler is a credible and reliable witness to the awful events that took place at my home and at Bryant's store. His testimony has been the same whether he was with me or speaking alone. Never have I had to question his account of the Emmett Till case.

1

Life in Mississippi

MISSISSIPPI IN THE 1950S, when I was coming of age, was just like Mississippi in the 1860s, when the Ku Klux Klan and night riders were part of our daily lives.

I was born October 15, 1942, in Doddsville, in Sunflower County, where Daddy was working at the time. I grew up in a Jim Crow society, where everything was segregated. Jim Crow is just a shorthand way of saying that we had separate schools, water fountains, cafes, churches, and restaurants. The *cemeteries* were segregated—it was even against the law for black and white dead people to be together. Our contact with white people was limited. And when there was contact, it was initiated by whites.

I recall one instance when a white plantation owner, Mr. Peterson, came to our home and asked if I could spend the day swimming with his son, Tommy. I was allowed to go only after I finished my chores. It was the last day of chopping cotton, and I was the last one in the field. Swimming with Tommy was great fun, but I felt a little uneasy swimming without any clothes on before white people. When swimming with my brothers, we always found a

Me at about six years old.

secluded spot. In the back of my mind, I kept wondering what the white folks were thinking as Tommy and I made all of that noise while they were fishing.

Tommy could come by whenever he wanted, but I was never allowed to meet with him on my own initiative. I was never allowed inside his home. The same kind of restrictions existed when the sons of the "straw bosses" (supervisors who often substituted for the real bosses) came to play with us. They always came to visit me; I never went to visit them.

We children were kept separated until they needed us.

Once, my mother told me that when Tommy became a man, I would have to call him mister. But he would never have to call me that. We were the same age, and I made up my mind then and there that I would never call him mister. This was one of my first real reactions to Jim Crow. But over the next few years, I had to learn the other unwritten laws of the South that my mother and father knew very well.

My sister Hallie had become real good friends with a white woman, and one day she took Hallie with her to Greenwood, the nearest large town. They were in town shopping and having a good time when the white woman decided she wanted some ice cream. She asked Hallie if she wanted some too. Hallie said yes, but the clerk behind the counter refused to sell the white woman any ice cream for Hallie. He was willing to sell it only if it was for her. They walked out of the store together without buying anything.

We faced a similar Jim Crow policy in our school system. "Separate but equal" was the name of the game. There was a white school near our home, but we were bussed to a school far across town with all black students and teachers. All we could do was look at the white school, with its merry-go-round, slides, swings, and other playthings. We had none of these things at the school I attended. Yes, we had a basketball court, but we had to dribble the ball on dirt. And believe me, we kicked up so much dust you could hardly tell when somebody had made a basket. Given the education we received in the classroom, where we were essentially trained to be farmers, we might as well have stayed on the basketball court.

The rules of separation were also in force at the three theaters in Greenwood. At the Paramount Theater, for example, downstairs was reserved for white patrons; we had to go upstairs to the balcony.

More hurtful still was the justice system. Whites could beat us, even murder us, and nothing was ever done about it. It wasn't unusual for white men to hire black women as cooks or domestics and then force them into sexual relationships, which is nothing more than rape. Very little was said or done about this. We had no rights in court, and only the boldest of blacks dared to bring a lawsuit against a white person.

Most of the residents where we lived were farmers and, to put it more directly, sharecroppers. Here is how share-cropping worked: A landowner would plant cotton in the spring, usually in April. The sharecroppers would live on the land and cultivate the cotton—what we called "chopping" cotton—and it would be harvested during the last week of August. The landowner would sell the cotton, take a share of the money to cover all his expenses, and split the remaining money fifty-fifty with the sharecroppers.

That means the land we lived on and worked did not belong to us. In fact, only about four or five blacks in our area were landowners. Prior to working as a sharecropper, my father often leased the land and grew his own crops to sell. He did this because he didn't want any white man bossing his children. He knew how mean the whites were toward the blacks in Mississippi. Dad made good cotton crops during his time of leasing. But he could never get the same price the white plantation owners got for their bales. The cotton buyers even stopped buying Dad's cotton because it was produced by a black man. There was no alternative but to find a white man to sell it. So Dad got out of the leasing business.

Dad started working as a sharecropper in Schlater, Mississippi, for a man named John Ware. My father found him to be a fair and decent man. He stayed with Mr. Ware from the mid-1930s to 1945. Mr. Ware never cheated Dad out of his earnings. But in 1945, he sold his plantation to another white man, Mr. McShane. When Dad met with the new owner, he knew right away that he couldn't trust him. Although Dad had children older than him, Mr. McShane talked to Dad as if Dad were only a boy. So Dad let him know that he wouldn't be working for him. Mr. McShane's reaction was to send word to Dad asking him to move out of the house where he lived. Dad said that he wasn't going to move until he found a new home for his family—and that until that happened, no one else was going to move in with him either. Even the messenger who had brought Mr. McShane's request, my brother-in-law Wheeler Parker Sr., was frightened by Dad's reply. He wasn't afraid for Dad, but he was afraid to deliver Dad's message to the boss man.

Dad then moved us to a town called Money, where he became a sharecropper for the same man he had leased land from prior to sharecropping. His name was Grover Frederick, and Dad trusted him.

Dad realized that he could not take on the Jim Crow system of injustice and inhumane treatment directly, and certainly not alone. So he stayed out of the way of those whites who were dishonest and particularly hateful toward blacks. He only worked for honest and decent men.

Unlike us, Dad also never worked as a hired hand for other plantations. One particular plantation where my brothers and I picked cotton used unjust scales that did not register the weight accurately. One hundred pounds of cotton, which I used to pick by noon, would weigh in at seventy pounds. This was the Mississippi plantation owners' way of stealing from the black man's labor, just as their forebears had done during slavery. We suspected this plantation used what was called a "loaded pee." The pee was a weight that slid up the scale until it was balanced. If the pee wasn't loaded, you got an honest measurement; if the pee was loaded, meaning extra weight was added to it secretly, a dishonest measurement was produced in favor of the plantation owner.

Instead, Dad worked his forty acres of cotton and took care of his two gardens and a garden belonging to Mr. Frederick. We had heard of horror stories about other families working all year as sharecroppers, only to be told, "Sorry, you didn't make any money this year." They were often told that not only were there no profits but that they had come out in the hole. "Your crop did not produce enough to cover your expenses" was another comment we heard quite a bit. If there was no profit, only a deficit, we wondered how the boss could take 50 percent of nothing and build his beautiful home. But none of this ever happened to Dad, mainly because he was very careful and particular about whom he worked for. Mr. Frederick was fair and Dad cleared money every year. Not once was he told that he had come out in the hole.

I'm not exactly sure how Dad was so perceptive when it came to dealing with white landowners; it may have stemmed from a deep-seated suspicion that he shared with many other black farmers, given what they had seen happen to their fathers and grandfathers.

Dishonest whites had long used such tactics to accumulate wealth, bolster their way of living, and maintain a segregated South. All you could do was endure it. You couldn't run away. The only way to do that was to buy a car, which very few of us could afford; if you had one, you'd better have enough gas to keep going until you were out of the South, because there were no motels or hotels that accommodated blacks.

Even on the trains there was segregation. To share the same coach with a white person was out of the question. We had to sit in a certain car, a certain part of the train, until it crossed the Mississippi River into Cairo, Illinois. Only then could we move about, go to another car, or sit where we chose. Blacks and whites used separate washrooms during the journey. Segregation was also enforced on the buses: whites in the front, blacks in the back. (Of course, since we lived out in the country and Dad owned a car, riding a bus was not a part of our daily routine.)

There were all sorts of other ways of keeping us in our place—impoverished, without power, and under their thumbs. Basically, we were not free, could not choose our own destiny, and might as well have been living in South Africa under the apartheid regime rather than in America, the so-called land of the free and home of the brave. In the eyes of most white southerners, we were less than human and really didn't count. If you didn't live in the Jim Crow South, you'd think it was a fantasy, a horrible fairy tale. But I lived there a good part of my youth, struggling against the unjust laws, the unfair separation, and the brutal treatment, and it was all too real.

Some may ask how white people in the South could keep black Americans in subjection for so long. The violent system of Jim Crow laws was backed by the intimidation of the Ku

Klux Klan, the White Citizens' Council, and other vicious segregationist groups. Any black person brave enough to violate this system was immediately confronted by angry white men, usually with murder on their minds. There was nothing more feared in the South than one of these lynch mobs, which was invariably protected by the sheriff and his deputies—when they weren't part of the mob themselves. For every courageous black man willing to speak out against the circumstances we faced, hundreds of white men were willing and able to make sure he paid the ultimate price. And when this form of injustice was supported by law enforcement officials—the sheriff and his deputies; the prosecutor or the judge—then the lynch mob knew it could murder a black man or woman without ever being brought to justice. So we "went along to git along," to quote an old saying.

I remember my father talking about the presidential elections in 1952, when Senator Adlai Stevenson of Illinois was running against General Dwight D. Eisenhower. We would listen to the news on the radio, and Dad was for Stevenson. He felt that the Democrats would give us a better deal than the Republicans. But no blacks went to vote. I wasn't aware at the time, but blacks were not allowed to vote unless they were able to overcome all kinds of obstacles, such as Jim Crows laws forcing them to pass literacy tests or pay poll taxes. Vernon Dahmer, who, I later learned, led black voter registration drives in Mississippi in the 1960s, used to say, "If you don't vote, you don't count." For that, he was killed by members of the Klan.

Not much has been written about Dahmer, but a few of the folks in Argo, the Chicago suburb where I later lived, often talked about him, since they had relatives in the same region of Mississippi. Dahmer owned a store where black residents could pay their two-dollar poll taxes. For this audacity the Klan firebombed and shot up his home in 1966. Dahmer was seriously wounded and died the next day. It was not until 1998 that Sam Bowers, an Imperial Wizard of the Klan, was convicted of this crime by a multiracial jury and sentenced to life in prison.

I wish it were possible to say something about *all* those courageous freedom fighters who risked their lives so that others would have the right to vote. A couple of them stand out in my memory and should get more than just a few passing words.

Just a week before my cousin Emmett Till—we called him Bobo—came to visit us in 1955, Lamar Smith was murdered in Brookhaven, in the southern part of Mississippi. A group of white men, who had warned him to stop helping black residents to vote, gunned him down right in front of the courthouse. As he lay dying, he was still clutching some election leaflets in his hands. Smith refused to knuckle under or to be intimidated by the white mobs who threatened him.

Three men were arrested for the murder, but they were never brought to trial. Smith was just another black man gone. From the newspapers we learned that Medgar Evers had gotten involved in the case, which didn't surprise us, since he was the field representative for the state's branch of the National Association for the Advancement of Colored People (NAACP). Dad had a lot of respect for him and the organization, but he knew they could only do so much against the Jim Crow system that controlled our lives.

In the spring, a few months earlier, the Reverend George Wesley Lee, who lived in Belzoni, not too far from us, was killed for his civil rights activism. Reverend Lee, like Dad, was a preacher who administered more than one congregation. He was also a very successful businessman and owner of a grocery store. The Klan had told him to remove his name from the voting rolls and to stop carrying out his campaign to register black voters. But Lee defied them. One evening he was driving home after picking up some clothes from the cleaners when a car filled with white men pulled up alongside him and blasted his car with three rounds of buckshot. The blast tore off half his face and sent the car careening into the front of a house. He staggered out of the crash but was dead on arrival at a nearby hospital. People talked about this case for quite a while, though no one was arrested for the crime. A grand jury was established to see if there were grounds for prosecution of the suspects, but it found none, an outcome that was expected. It was a rare day indeed when a white man was convicted of killing a black man, even a minister.

This deeply affected Dad. If they would kill a man of God, someone whose only interest was to spread the Word and to comfort the sick, then nobody's life was safe.

These murders and an untold number of other lynchings were part of our daily lives. Most black people where we lived had grown accustomed to the Klan and other night riders. It was the kind of powerlessness that kept folks in their place; even so, there were exceptions to the rule, and I think the Reverend George Lee, Lamar Smith, and Medgar Evers were cut from a different mold. Dad, too, was like them, and he might have done more if he hadn't feared jeopardizing his large family if he became too outspoken.

When we finally gained access to the ballot box, things began to change. Now whites began to worry and to complain about how things were changing, and they were fearful that the power they had would gradually disappear. Even more astonishing, they charged *us* with being the racists, claimed that *we* were the bigoted and prejudiced ones. Most of us knew it was useless debating the issue. Nowadays you hear a lot about reverse discrimination. But this may have been the very beginning of that kind of talk, right in the heart of Ku Klux Klan land.

And then there was the Supreme Court's 1954 decision, in *Brown v. Board of Education*, to outlaw segregation in the schools. Mississippi, like so many other southern states, seemed to have a thick immunity to laws or judgments that would dare to promote integration. There were times when we could play with white kids, but going to school with them was another thing. Jim Crow had been around so long that even in his old age there were some things that he was not about to relinquish, not about to change.

One of the signs posted in Mississippi read: "Nigger read and run, and if you can't read, run anyway." There were places where warnings such as "Don't let the sun go down on you in this town" were commonplace, and the majority of black residents knew exactly what they meant. They were not about to violate the written or unwritten laws of white supremacy.

This was the way things had been for more than a hundred years, and after a while your reaction was second nature. You didn't have to think about getting off the sidewalk when a white person came your way; you did it automatically, instinctively. It was "Yes, sir," and "No, sir"; no ifs, ands, or buts about it. To step outside these codes was to risk your life. The nature of white violence was ingrained in us, and only the bold and the foolish challenged the system. We knew our place and after being in it for so many years, enduring the slights, insults, and disrespect, we learned how to be comfortable with that degrading lot. Most of us just bided our time until we could see a better opportunity to exercise our resistance to the system.

Sure, there were stories and tales about some brave blacks who stood up to "Mr. Charlie," as the white man was called. But in the end, the black resistor was the victim and the white man who insulted, whipped, or murdered him went scot-free—and was later praised for standing up to preserve the racist system. Supreme Court justice Roger Taney had made it clear way back in 1857 in the *Dred Scott* case that the black man had no rights the white man was bound to respect, and that was that.

This was the kind of system that still prevailed in the state in 1955, when Bobo came down from Chicago to visit us for the last time.

2

My Family

MY DAD, MOSES "MOSE" WRIGHT, was born April 9, 1892. This wasn't a good time to be born in Mississippi, particularly for a black farmer, though it's hard to think when would have been a good time for a black person to be born in a racist state. Later, I learned that Dad shared a birthday with the great singer Paul Robeson, who was born six years later. Dad often spoke of his admiration for Robeson and his commitment to ending racial injustice.

Dad used to talk about growing up without a mother. Basically, he was raised by his father. When it came to race relations, Grandpa Billy was a man ahead of his time. He let it be known that he did not want any white man bossing his children around. Dad would express a similar outlook about me and my siblings.

I am not sure if Grandpa actually owned the land where he lived, but that's the impression I have gotten from my uncles. He may have been among the hundreds of black farmers of the time who in fact owned large plots of land. Many black farmers had worked this land during slavery times, so they knew how fertile it was and how profitable it could be. By the time my grandpa was coming of age in the mid-1870s, black farmers must have owned two-thirds of the land in the Delta. Many of them had acquired the land because the white owners had abandoned it ahead of the invading Union Army during the Civil War. And many of them held on despite the fall of the price of cotton, which was the main product grown in the region. Of course, by the time Dad came along, things had begun to change dramatically because of the Depression in the 1920s and 1930s, and many black farmers had to sell their land to pay their debts. But my uncle Jackson's daughters still own land in Lexington, Mississippi, and my uncle Will's children own over sixty acres in Browning, which is not too far from Greenwood. Dad always regretted selling his land.

In 1908, when Dad was sixteen, he ran away from home because of a misunderstanding with Grandpa. Dad told us that one Sunday after a church social he walked two girls home. He said he was floating "in a mist," in seventh heaven. But Grandpa was not excited about this. When Dad got home, Grandpa hit him and knocked him down. I never did get a full explanation of what happened between them. But to get away, Dad ran and hid alongside a road. From there, Dad said he could hear Grandpa say, "If he's gone, he better stay gone. If he comes back here, I am going to kill him."

Dad realized the danger he faced if he returned home right away, so he went to Durant, just a little to the east of Lexington, Mississippi, and right on the Big Black River in Holmes County. After a while he got a job working for a black farmer in the vicinity. From this job he secured the trust of other farmers in the region, all of whom respected him for his honesty. Unfortunately, Dad never got a chance to attend his father's funeral. When Dad was finally notified that his father was dead, it was too late. He told me that his younger brother Jackson, who was responsible for getting him the message, failed to inform him in time.

Three years after Dad left home, in 1911, he married his first wife, Lucinda Larry, whom he had met after he settled in Durant. To this union was born four children: Willie Mae, James, Cornelius, and Hallie Mae. Lucinda was very devout, and this had a great impact on Dad. The first years of their marriage, Dad would stay out all night on Friday and Saturday night. He would come home smelling like alcohol, but his dear wife never complained or scolded him for that. After a while Dad vowed that he would never mistreat her again, and committed his life to Christ. Soon he began to travel throughout Mississippi as a so-called CC rider, or country-circuit preacher, preaching the word of the Gospel in those godforsaken places where small congregations thirsted after the Word of the Lord. His ability to move a congregation to ecstasy and emotional outbursts with his preaching became the talk of the region.

In 1917 Dad was drafted into the army, but he refused to go. This was the same year that the government passed the Selective Service Act, authorizing federal conscription for the armed forces—suddenly, all males between the ages of twenty-one and thirty had to register for the draft. The act followed shortly behind President Woodrow Wilson's resolution to enter World War I to make the world "safe for democracy," which Dad insisted didn't exist in Mississippi.

By this time Dad had been a preacher of the Gospel for a year and strongly believed that fighting was wrong. He was arrested and jailed for thirty days. He declared that he would rather die than fight in World War I. If he was given any special consideration because he was a minister, he never told us, but there were at least five different classifications of draft eligibility, and members of the clergy were classified as exempt. Nevertheless, for this action he became quite a celebrity, and people from all around the county and the surrounding towns would come to see this black man who had made such a statement. I don't think there were many draft dodgers or resisters in the Delta, but Dad stuck by his guns, and he was determined not to pick one up for the army. After he was released, he resumed his traveling about Mississippi, preaching the Gospel.

People often ask me if Dad was a pacifist and what motivated him to resist the draft. He was a member of the Church of God in Christ, an upstart denomination that stressed holiness and the baptism of the Holy Spirit and that felt it was wrong for brothers to kill one another. The church's founder, Charles Harrison Mason—Bishop Mason, as he was known—went to jail for preaching against military service. It appears Dad heeded Bishop Mason's call and refused to obey his draft notice on the grounds of religious conviction.

Dad's wife, Lucinda, died in 1921, apparently from the flu pandemic that had ravaged the vicinity a few years before. In fact, there were some 20 million cases of influenza and pneumonia in the United States in 1918–1919. Approximately 850,000 cases were fatal, and Camp Shelby, Mississippi, was one of the areas devastated by the pandemic. Right after Lucinda's death, Dad sold his land. The burden of caring for it while being responsible for raising his first four children, together with his commitment to spreading the Word of the Lord, was too much to handle.

My mother, Elizabeth Smith, was born in 1900; her granddad was Mr. Haley, a white slave owner. She was raised

Bobo's father, Louis Till (seated). He appears to be wearing the ring later given to Bobo, the one that was used to identify his body.

in the little town of Hazlehurst, Mississippi, and her family later moved to another small Mississippi town, Sumner. Mom had seven brothers and two sisters. Her older sister was my aunt Mamie (Smith Hall), and her younger sister was Alma (Smith Spearman), who was Bobo's grandmother.

Bobo's mother was born in 1921 to Aunt Alma and her husband at the time, John Nash Carthan. Alma named her only daughter Mamie Elizabeth, after her sisters. The family moved from Sumner to Chicago in 1924, when Mamie was two years old. Later, when they moved to Argo, Illinois, Mamie met Louis Till of New Madrid, Missouri, whom she married in 1940 when she was eighteen. I have in my possession an *Argo Starch Plant Newspaper*, in which this conversation appeared between Louis Till and his boss:

Till: "Can I have Friday off?" Boss: "Why?" Till: "Well, I have some business downtown I have to take care of." Boss: "Is it important business?" Till: "I've got to get a marriage license." Boss: "Well, well, and who is she?" Till: "Mamie Elizabeth Carthan of Argo. We expect to get married right away."

Bobo was born the following year, on July 25, 1941. His father died in 1945, when Bobo was not quite four years old. Bobo and I were, as they say, first cousins once removed.

Bobo and his mother.

As for my mother, for a period of time she lived in Memphis, Tennessee, where she had gone to teach school. In 1925 she returned to Sumner to marry Dad, whom she had met when he was the guest speaker at a church service she attended.

My uncles were worried about Dad marrying such a light-skinned woman. Many of the white people who didn't know them would look at them funny, perhaps wondering what this black man was doing with a white woman. Just about every state in the South had laws prohibiting marriages across the color line. And in New York, the same year Mom and Dad got married, the famous Rhinelander case was centered on a black woman accused of duping a white man by passing as white. Several novels from the Harlem Renaissance era were based on "passing." I don't know if

Mose Wright, my father.

Dad was conscious of all these developments, but he certainly knew some of the hazards of having a light-skinned wife, especially in a state where black men were lynched for merely looking at a white woman, to say nothing of speaking to or whistling at one.

Mom made it clear to my father before they married that she didn't know how to pick cotton and didn't plan on doing it. On a couple of occasions she tried, but she couldn't stand the heat. She was not a very big woman—a little less than five feet tall—but she was quite sturdy. At that time, she was mainly a housewife, content to take care of a large family. I was the last of her eight children, coming into the world behind Moses Jr., George Arthur, Thelma, Loretha, Willie

Elizabeth Wright, my mother.

Crosby, Maurice, and Robert. Counting the children Dad had by his first wife, I had eleven brothers and sisters in all.

For the most part, Mom and Dad got along pretty well. She never called him Moses or Mose; she always addressed him as Preacher. Most of the people who knew Dad called him Preacher Wright. Dad called Mom by her pet name, Mack. I'm not sure where he got that one.

My mother always wanted the best for her children. She and my father had a system whereby one of them seemed to always be home with us. And she would often talk about moving from Mississippi to Chicago, where she believed there were greater opportunities for blacks. Another reason was to follow her brothers and sisters, almost all of whom had relocated there. Dad would not budge. He said that he loved Mississippi, that he was born and raised in Mississippi, and that he planned on dying there. I am sure many whites had plans to fulfill that last of his desires.

Mom and Dad had their arguments and disagreements, but Dad always came out on top. This might have been because Mom recognized Dad as the man of the house and to keep a sense of harmony, it was easier to let him have his way than continue to protest and argue. But these disagreements were mild and never resulted in fights. Our family was blessed and without any real disturbance until that fateful day in 1955.

3

At Home with Mom and Dad

I WAS THREE YEARS OLD when my family moved from Schlater to the little town of Money. Actually, we lived on a stretch of land called East Money, which was isolated from the town itself. East Money was approximately seven miles long east to west and about a mile and a half from north to south, and it was accessible only by County Road 542, a lonely, ominous byway that we called Dark Fear Road. If you ventured down that road at night, you would see why—it was one of the darkest places in the world, filled with menacing woods and snake-infested lakes. But old-timers say it also got its name from the many lynchings that took place in the area.

By the summer of 1955, when I was twelve years old, our four-bedroom house on Dark Fear Road was home to me, Mom, Dad, my fourteen-year-old brother Robert, and my sixteen-year-old brother Maurice. Our house had been the home of the boss man, Mr. Frederick, before he built himself a new one, and it wasn't the typical shack—we had a screened front porch that covered the width of the house. The four bedrooms were arranged in a square, and you could enter the house through either of the front bedrooms—each had a door. On the right as you entered were the two guest rooms. Mom and Dad's bedroom was the first room on the left, and directly behind their room was our bedroom. Maurice, Robert, and I slept in the same room—it was large enough to accommodate two beds. It was also convenient for Dad: when it was time to wake us up, he didn't have to go to the other rooms.

From our room a door led to the back of the house; a storage closet separated our room from the dining room. At the very back of the house sat the kitchen. On the side of the house, along the kitchen and dining room, was another porch; there was a third porch in back of the rear guest room.

Our house was raised on cinder blocks because of the annual flooding of Lake Never-Fail, the lake across the road from our house. We didn't have a boat, but there was always one in front of the house that our neighbor owned. Speaking of water, we got ours from a well about a half block away. The spigot ran continuously and never shut off, the pool overflowing into a ditch that found its way into Lake Never-Fail. And it was fresh water. We used buckets to carry it from the well. We had to haul water from the well every day, because we needed it for cooking, bathing, drinking, and household cleaning.

Mom was always the first to get up in the morning so she could prepare the fire in the stove for cooking. We had biscuits for breakfast every morning—that's what Dad wanted and that's what he got. A typical day at our house began with all of us at the breakfast table.

I can never remember my dad being around the house after he had eaten his breakfast. He was not the kind of man who would spend much time lying or sitting around. It seems he was always doing something or on his way to doing something. Somehow, some way, he found something to keep him busy. He was sixty-three in 1955, and many people thought he was my grandfather, but he still had a lot of energy—he was always working in his garden or for the boss man down the road from us. I never knew him to be sick. There is an old expression in the South about a man like Dad. They say, "He had a lot of get-up-and-go," and he certainly did.

I was very close to my father, probably the closest of the children. He would watch us like a hawk in the cotton fields, making sure we did our share and didn't waste a lot of time throwing cotton bolls at each other. His orders were to keep your head down and your hands moving.

Mom, on the other hand, was the sweetest and most easygoing person I knew. She was so easy that one time we went to her and asked, "Mom, when are you going to whip us?" Of course, we never asked Dad that question. Dad gave me every whipping he promised me—and a couple whippings that he did not.

I was about six or seven years old when I got my first whipping from Dad. It happened after I had finished taking a bath in a number-three tin tub, in which you mainly stood up to bathe, since it wasn't that big and you had to fold yourself in a knot to fit inside of it. Whenever we bathed, all the children used the same water, and since I was the youngest, I was the last of the children to bathe. (Daddy and my mother would bathe in separate water.) Anyway, the tub was in the room that would later become the front guest bedroom (but at the time belonged to my sister Loretha). It was also the room where the fireplace was located. While I was taking a bath, I got cold. There was some kerosene next to the fireplace, and so I took the container and dumped some of it on the fire. Suddenly, with a roar, the flames shot up through the chimney and the soot in the chimney caught on fire. It was roaring like a freight train, and I was scared the house was going to burn down.

The fire caused such a commotion that my mother and dad came running into the room to see what had happened. When Mom realized what I had done, she put me in some long white drawers and nothing else. She told me, "Boy, you better get out of here." I took off running down through the cotton fields, and Daddy was right behind me with a switch. All the neighbors watched as I ran as fast as I could. But I was not fast enough. One smack on my behind and the race was over.

I remember another whipping around the same time, after I took some money from my neighbor's pants pockets and bought me a pack of Kool cigarettes. Dad didn't know I smoked, but I would sneak off and do it. He didn't smoke anything and he didn't chew tobacco like a lot of the farmers in our town. Later in life he drank a little wine to soothe what he believed was a bladder problem. But this didn't amount to more than a sip every now and then.

I never witnessed Dad confronting a white man, but I did see him stand up against a young black man, the late Wes Carthen, who came to our house to beat up my brother Maurice. This guy was really big and we felt he would hurt Maurice, so we ran and told Daddy. Daddy ran in the house and got his 12-gauge shotgun and waited on the porch. When the young man arrived, Daddy asked him, "You tired of living?"

He said, "No, sir."

"Well, you'd better get out of my yard," Daddy told him. He turned around and hurried on up the road. Years later Wes and I laughed about that incident.

Daddy never fired that shotgun unless he was out hunting. Sometimes he would bring home some rabbits. But we caught more rabbits with sticks and our dog, Dallas, than he did with his gun. Rabbits can only run so far before they tire out, and then we would catch up to them and capture them.

We got most of our meat from the hogs and chickens we raised. We had chickens all over the place, and every Sunday we had chicken with our breakfast and evening meal. When it came to snapping a chicken's neck, my mother could do it as well as anyone. She would then chop off the head. I have never found anyone to come close to how my mother could cook a chicken. We also had all the eggs we could eat, and we would sell some of them to the boss man.

Whenever I talk about chickens, people want to know where we got them. It was the same way we got most of our household goods—from out of a catalog. That's right, the chickens came through the mail. Every winter Dad would order them from Sears, located in Memphis. One of the real challenges my parents faced was keeping the biddies, the baby chicks, alive. If they survived the first three weeks, there was a good chance they would live long enough to end up on a plate.

Every November was hog-killing time. All the neighbors would come around to help us slaughter the hogs. To
kill the hog you hit it in the head with an axe. Then you
dipped it in hot water, let it sit for a while, and trimmed all
the hair from the hide. Until we purchased our first refrigerator in 1953, we treated the meat with salt and special pre-
servatives and placed it in a small storehouse so it would last
through the winter months. We ate just about everything on
the hog, including the brains, which Daddy loved scrambled
with some eggs. We made our own sausage; I hardly eat sausage today because it doesn't compare to the homemade stuff
I enjoyed in Mississippi. Dad was a great provider and we
never missed a meal.

For our desserts, we often had blueberry or blackberry
pie. The blueberries grew along the road and the railroad
track, and we would pick them and sell them back to Dad
for thirty cents a quart. Of course, we also helped Dad eat
the pie, so we got double enjoyment from the dessert. On
special occasions, Mom would make two or three kinds of
cake, some of them triple layered. And all of this cooking was
done on a wood-burning stove. Even today I have no idea
how that stove worked.

Mom and Dad believed it was important that we get at
least a high school education. They never mentioned college.
Dad never said we had to go to school, but he had a saying: "You might not go to school, but you are leaving here."

Bobo shortly before his final visit.

I figured that since I couldn't hang around the house I may as well go on to school.

My father was self-taught and had a thorough understanding of the Bible. The day he committed his life to Christ, he sat down and read the New Testament from beginning to end. He had even been the pastor of his own church, the East Money Church of God in Christ, until he retired from pastoring in 1949.

Daddy was a sharp dresser, with several suits and lots of shirts that he had washed and ironed in Greenwood. Most of the pictures of him in books and newspapers show him in the clothes that he wore to the cotton fields, not in his Sunday best. Except for in those few photos and film clips, he always wore a hat. I didn't own a hat at the time, but Maurice had a black straw hat that had been given to him by our sister Loretha's boyfriend, Huey Lee, when they came down to visit us in July 1955. Bobo also liked to wear hats, and that's evident in one of the photos of him that was widely published. There's also a photo of Bobo when he was five, and even at that age he was a stylish dresser, thanks to his mother.

His hat is cocked just a little bit to the side, just the way he would wear it in later years.

When we bought new clothes, we would order them out of a Sears catalog, which gave us better deals than the white stores in Greenwood. I will never forget flipping the pages of the catalog and looking at all the beautiful shoes, pants, and other clothes we would order as a new school year began. The catalog was big and bulky with lots of pictures of just about everything imaginable. I loved thumbing through it, looking at the toys, all of which seemed so pretty and brand new. But I knew we were not rich, so owning some of them one day was just a dream I had.

We did own a small electric Philco radio, and a battery-operated one that didn't work too well. We would listen to *Ernie's Record Parade* and *The Grand Ole Opry* out of Nashville, Tennessee. We also listened to the Friday-night boxing matches—I remember Rocky Marciano defending his heavyweight title, or hearing how Sugar Ray Robinson or Joe Louis was beating somebody to a pulp. Of all of the sports figures of that time, Joe Louis was our favorite. He got paid to do something that many other black men only dreamed of—to get in a boxing ring and whip a white man. He and Sugar Ray Robinson showed us a brand-new world for blacks outside of Mississippi. Although we suffered under the Jim Crow system in the South, they gave us hope. I could see that there was a different world out there.

We also had a record player, but my mother only played gospel music; there were no jazz or blues records around our house. We could hear blues and stuff on the radio, musicians such as Muddy Waters, John Lee Hooker, and Ruth Brown, but they could never be heard on her record player. We couldn't even whistle in Mose's house. If you wanted to whistle, you had to go outside. And there was no cursing allowed in our house either.

After a long day completing his chores, Dad would sit on the front porch for a while, and my mother often sat with him, especially in the evening after supper, talking about what happened that day. Dad was mostly interested in two things: his cotton patches and politics. Even before the Great Depression, cotton and politics were topics on everybody's mind, especially after acres and acres of farmland were destroyed in the Mississippi River flood of 1927. Many were hurt by the flood, but Dad fared better than most because of his income from the churches where he was a pastor. Still, the flood had a ripple effect throughout the region, and things got even worse with the stock market crash. It was bad enough during the "good times" in Mississippi, but the Depression along with the rampant racism made life almost intolerable for black farmers and their families.

For her part, my mother would discuss what she had read in the paper. We subscribed to the *Commercial Appeal*, a white-owned newspaper out of Memphis, which came through the mail five days a week. There were other papers, but Dad and Mom preferred the *Appeal*, because they felt it wasn't as racist as the others. It's still in print today, and it continues to be very moderate in its political views. Both my parents kept up with the latest news, but I think my mother read a lot more. Daddy used to get mad at me and Robert because we would beat him to the paper, but we were looking for the comics section. *Joe Palooka, Dick Tracy, Mutt & Jeff, Buz Sawyer, Steve Roper,* and *Terry and the Pirates* were my favorites. Only on the sports page did we see a black face, unless some black person had been accused of a crime, killed somebody, or was killed himself.

I remember seeing articles in the *Commercial Appeal* about Eddie Nolan, a black man from Lexington, Mississippi, who wounded ten white men. This happened in 1950 or 1951; I'm not exactly sure about the date, but I know it was during the Korean War. First Nolan shot a white man who was seeing his wife, fled the scene, and found a hiding place in the woods. The white men who pursued him didn't know that he was a sharpshooter with a rifle, one of the best in the state. Over the next few days, each time a group of them came close to capturing him, he would pick them off one by one.

Finally, after he had wounded quite a few of his pursuers, they convinced him to surrender. But rather than lynching him, they spread the word that Nolan was crazy. This was done because they didn't want any other black men to get the same idea.

My mother kept up with crime stories and news reports related to law and order, and she often talked about a white man named Hawkjaw Mullin and his bloodhounds. Whenever a prisoner escaped from jail or prison, Mullin would be summoned to track him down and return him to custody. Like the North-West Canadian Mounties, Hawkjaw had a reputation of always getting his man, no matter how long it took.

Mom also dwelled on the danger we children faced coming of age in Mississippi. She often warned us never to walk on a frozen lake, and we were told to refrain from smoking and using drugs. Then there was her fear of us being kidnapped. This stemmed from her reading about the kidnapping of the Lindbergh baby in the spring of 1932, almost ten years before I was born. We were spellbound listening to Mom as she told us how the Lindbergh baby was kidnapped and the fifty thousand dollars in ransom was paid, but the family never got the child back. The baby's mutilated body was found about two months later. Mom said that they finally caught a man named Bruno Hauptmann, who was tried, found guilty, and put in the electric chair about four years after the kidnapping. All of this happened in New Jersey, so even outside of Mississippi, kidnapping was a danger. Little did I know that soon I would be sharing in the same horror the Lindbergh family had suffered in 1932. I wonder if Mom sensed that one day we too would be victims of a kidnapping and murder.

By the summer of 1955, most of our attention was focused on the upcoming arrival of my nephews Wheeler Parker Jr. (sixteen-year-old son of my sister Hallie) and Curtis Jones (seventeen-year-old son of my oldest sister, Willie Mae) and my fourteen-year-old cousin Bobo. (We didn't know that Bobo's real first name was Emmett until after he was killed.) Dad had gone to Chicago to speak at the funeral of one of his old parishioners, and he was bringing Bobo and Wheeler back with him for a visit; Curtis, who was on the train with them, was coming to visit his aunt in Greenwood. I was beside myself with excitement. It was beyond gladness—it was pure joy.

One of my greatest thrills was to have relatives visit us from the North. Every summer someone from "up north" came down to visit us. We had a lot of company in 1955: July was when my sister Loretha and her boyfriend came down to visit, and my brother Willie came home on leave from the army that year—he had just finished basic training at Fort Leonard Wood, Missouri.

It didn't matter whether visiting relatives were old or young. I looked forward to the stories they would tell, the information about their lives. Everything about them was different—the clothes they wore, the way they talked. Bobo had visited us once before, when he was about six years old. The only thing about that visit that I remember is that he came down with an earache. He seemed to be in such pain. Bobo and I had met again two years later, when I visited Chicago with my mom, but by now it had been six years since I'd seen him. I had a thousand questions ready to spring on him, and I knew he was prepared to answer all of them. I also wondered what he looked like now. Was he taller than I was; was he still full of life? What about Chicago? Was it true that you could walk up and down South Water Street Market, the produce capital of Chicago, and have your pick of all kinds of fruit? Was Riverview Park as big as Maurice had said? Maurice had gone to Chicago more recently, in 1954, and he tried to explain to us about South Water Market and Riverview, but I wanted to hear what Bobo had to say. Everybody knew that when Bobo arrived, he would be the center of attention, and I couldn't wait to have him all to myself.

But before he got there, we had a lot of cleaning and other things to do to make sure his stay with us was comfortable. The guest bedrooms were made ready. Mom assigned the sleeping arrangements. Bobo, Robert, and I would sleep in the bedroom behind theirs. Wheeler would share the front guest room with Maurice. Wheeler had actually lived next door to us before he moved to Argo in 1947. He was visiting us for the first time since leaving eight years ago.

I also made plans for how we would beat the heat. Swimming was high on the agenda, and going to Greenwood was a must. Bobo would arrive on a Saturday, and I knew that the following Monday I would be in the cotton field; that was the beginning of the cotton harvest. We'd have little time to spend with each other. We had no time to waste.

4

The Abduction

IT WAS SATURDAY, AUGUST 20, and Maurice had driven to the train station in Grenada, Mississippi, to pick up Dad, Wheeler, and Bobo. I was so excited that I didn't know what to do. I kept my eyes on the road looking for their arrival in Dad's 1946 Ford sedan. Dark Fear Road was gravel, and you could see cars approaching at least a mile away from the dust that would be billowing up from behind. Finally they arrived, Maurice parking the car in the front yard (while Dad could drive, he often deferred to someone else). Dad was the first to exit the car. When Bobo got out, his size was the first thing I noticed. He was quite big for a fourteen-year-old: he must have weighed about 140 pounds and was a little over five foot six; at twelve, I weighed about 90 pounds and was just five feet tall.

You could say that he was chubby, with big, round hazel eyes and sandy hair. He was wearing what we called a Sunday hat—a little out of place on the farm—khaki pants, and a short-sleeved cotton shirt. His shirt was not like the nylon shirts we wore—you know, the ones you can see your undershirt through. There was something else that caught my eye: he had on a silver ring with the initials *LT* on it—his father's initials. I admired it so much that Bobo let me wear it for a couple of days. I was later able to identify that same ring that was taken off Bobo's body.

On Sunday, Bobo wanted to go up to Money to buy some fireworks. You could buy fireworks in town at any time of the year. Maurice drove us there, and Bobo bought some fireworks from Mr. Wolf's, one of five stores in the small town. I thought that we were going to go back home and then set them off. To our dismay, Bobo lit some of the firecrackers in front of the store. I told him that you could not set off firecrackers within the city limits. He wasn't trying to be funny—he just didn't know the rules.

The next day was the start of the cotton harvest on our sharecropper farm. It was a typically bright Mississippi morning, when the August ground is blistering hot hours before breakfast is even served. There was general excitement around our house, not just because this was the first day of the harvest but also because Bobo was with us.

Bobo had kept me up the night before, telling me all kinds of stories and describing what it was like in Chicago now that the weather was changing. I enjoyed the sound of his voice; when Bobo talked, he stuttered, and more so when he got excited, but he used that to capture your attention. I asked him what he would be doing at home if he hadn't come to visit us. He said he would probably be having fun with his other friends up there. Summers in Chicago, he told me, were wonderful, and he really enjoyed going to Lincoln Park, where there were rides, picnics, swimming, and a variety of other outdoor events. I fell asleep that night and dreamed of Chicago and playing in the park with Bobo and his friends.

We were aroused from slumber by the sound of my father's whistling. This was a sure sign that he was in a good mood and eager to get the harvesting underway. He had finished the last of his early chores just as we gulped down the last of our grits, eggs, and bacon. A few minutes earlier he had placed a fresh bucket of milk on the side porch, so we knew he had just milked the cows. Before that task he usually fed the dozen or so squealing hogs and "watered" the chickens. With each completed chore his whistling got louder. And then there was the whistle for us to make it snappy. "Let's go, boys." Dad had a saying: "Let's go back, let's go back—the work ain't hard and the man ain't mean." "We've got a long day in front of us," he told us as we snatched up our sacks and tucked a few biscuits in our pockets.

This cotton-picking business would be a new ordeal for Bobo. Only after he pleaded with my father were he and Wheeler allowed to join us picking the cotton. These two city boys thought it would be fun. If they only knew, I thought, suppressing a chuckle. I knew the cotton field as well as the back of my hand—a hand, I might add, that had been picking the bolls since I was very young. I was eight years old when I began dragging a seven-foot sack through the fields behind me; at age twelve you were given a nine-footer. (It wasn't an unusual practice for cotton pickers to throw dirt and rocks into their sacks to make them heavier, particularly at the end of the day, when it was time to weigh them to see how much money you had coming. This surely goes back to slavery times, when captive Africans used all sorts of tricks to outwit their tormentors. But we would not dare do that with Dad's cotton.) That day, when Bobo and Wheeler were given nine-foot-long sacks to fill, the expression on their faces suddenly changed. A little bit of a smile returned when my father told them they could keep all the money they made. The pay was two dollars per hundred pounds, which wasn't exactly city-type money, but it was something.

Earning money didn't seem necessary for Bobo; he seemed always to have a pocketful of change, given to him mainly by his grandparents and great-grandparents. He was an only child, so he was showered with affection and money. The way he dressed reflected his good fortune and upbringing. While the rest of us wore overalls and blue jeans, Bobo wore dress pants or khaki trousers, and that silver ring of his. He was a sight to see in the cotton field, dressed like he was on his way to a party. He even had a pair of penny loafers, which was unheard of in the black neighborhood. To the rest of us who had to run errands and do other jobs for a nickel or two, money seemed to be at Bobo's disposal.

Around ten-thirty that first morning, the sun lingered above us. Sweat began to pour down Bobo's face. I could tell that this wasn't his kind of work. After plucking the cotton bolls from three or four rows of the spiky vine, Bobo's pace became slower and slower. At the rate he was going, I knew it would take a couple of hours before his sack would show any bulge of cotton.

That evening, after his first day in the field, Bobo told my mother, "Aunt Lizzie, it's too hot, and I can't stand the heat." My mother passed this on to my father, who permitted him to hang up his cotton sack and officially retire from the task. Of course, I was not allowed such mercy. That was only available to out-of-town guests and favorite cousins.

It was Monday evening, August 22, 1955. After we had supper, we kids decided to visit friends who lived along Dark

Fear Road. About ten of us assembled near the East Money Church of God in Christ, about a mile from our house. A couple of the boys were from the O'Neal plantation. One of them had a gun. As we were talking and hanging out, up drove a seventeen-year-old black boy named Fletcher and a friend. When Fletcher, who lived on Mr. Carter's place just south of Money, heard about the gun, he threatened to take it from whoever had it. Suddenly there was silence. The only thing you could hear were crickets and a few frogs croaking. No one dared speak up, and Fletcher's challenge went unheeded. Fletcher wasn't a big fellow, but he was mean as a snake. Also, he drove a tractor for Mr. Carter, and because of this job he felt that he could do anything he wanted to another black and get away with it. I asked my friend at the last school reunion whatever happened to Fletcher. He told me that Fletcher was serving time at Parchman Farm, the notorious Mississippi state prison.

Bobo was stunned by everyone's inability to stand up to Fletcher. Because he was an outsider, he didn't feel a need to say anything at the time, but after it was over, he let us have it. From his perspective, we had no backbone. Under a bluff from a bully, we had tucked tail and run. I've never forgotten how upset he was with us, particularly me, who was his flesh and blood. "How can you let someone come on your turf and strut his stuff?" he snapped. "You can't allow anyone to come around and disrespect you like that. We would never tolerate this in Chicago. What are you, a bunch of chickens?"

This was Bobo's personality—no one is to strut his stuff on your turf. Rule number one: "You cover the ground that you stand on." Like his clothing, it set him apart from the rest of us. I can still see him standing there now, with his soft, sandy hair and big hazel-colored eyes, and hear him express his dismay at us. He was always looking for ways to make us laugh, but in this case he wanted us to cover the ground we stood on, as he would do in Chicago.

I believe if he had lived, he would have been a great comedian. He knew the routines of all the top ones on television— Red Skelton, Jack Benny, Abbott and Costello, and George Gobel. Gobel, with his deadpan delivery, was a particular favorite of Bobo's. And it was that George Gobel expression he had on his face as he chastised us for our cowardice.

I could hear the spunk in his voice, an attitude of defiance and boldness that was not easy for me or any of us to express. Growing up in racist Mississippi, our voices had been muted. There was the unwritten rule of the plantation, at least for good workers: "If you stay out of the grave, I will keep you out of the jail." We had seen too often the brutal outcome for those who dared to speak out. Our place in the world was second class, and silence in the face of danger was expected.

After he finished bawling us out and calling us all kind of names, there was nothing else for us to do but go home and get a good night's sleep.

The next day, Tuesday, Bobo stayed home from the cotton fields, weary but wiser after his one-day baptismal in one of the South's oldest and most laborious activities. He was lucky but had nothing to do that day. He was so glad when we got home that evening. Since it had been boring for him, when we finished supper, he was eager for all of us to pile into the car and drive around. My brother Maurice was behind the wheel with the rest of us—me, Bobo, Wheeler, and my other brother Robert—talking and making as much noise as the engine. Someone, I don't remember who, came up with the idea of raiding a watermelon patch not too far from the county road. Maurice parked the car and we crept in. Each of us "borrowed" a good-sized melon and headed down to the riverbank.

We busted the melons, dug out the hearts, and began our feast. The heart of the watermelon was the sweetest and biggest section. It stuck up like a hill rising from the plain. If you cut the watermelon you would cut the heart in half; by busting it the heart stays attached to one of the half sections. Bobo was clearly enjoying himself. We Mississippi boys wanted very much for our cousins from up north to have a good time. He was very impressed with our swimming routine: we would run the snakes out of the water before we entered.

On Wednesday, August 24, there was no change in the routine. Bobo stayed home with my mother, while the rest of us grabbed our sacks and headed for the cotton patch. When we returned from another hard day in the field, Bobo again was jubilant. That day it had taken us a little longer because of the slowness at the cotton-sack weighing. But now, with the day behind us and dusk settling in, we all sat down to a scrumptious meal, exchanging stories about our time spent apart. Once more, to satisfy a restless Bobo, we were going to go out. We decided to drive up to Money again.

Again, Maurice was driving the old Ford, with Wheeler in the front seat along with one of our neighbors. I was in the backseat with Bobo and another neighbor. (My brother Robert wasn't with us this time.) The six of us kept up a steady stream of chatter all the way into town. The sun had just about disappeared over the horizon as we pulled into Money.

When we arrived, we went directly to Bryant's grocery store. It and the other four storefronts in town faced the east, and behind them ran the muddy Tallahatchie River. The name of the river is from the Choctaw Indian word meaning "rock of waters." I remember it as a turbulent, menacing river

Bryant's grocery store.

with a strong current. It was too dangerous to swim in, so we always kept our distance.

As we reached Bryant's store, we continued our usual small talk and banter. We were still excited about the day's events and happy to be in town together. We all got out of the car and were milling around in the front of the store when Wheeler went in to buy a pop or some candy. Bobo went in after him; then Wheeler came out, leaving Bobo in there alone.

Maurice immediately sent me into the store to be with Bobo. He was concerned about Bobo being in the store alone because of what had happened on the previous Sunday, when Bobo had set his fireworks off inside the city limits. He just didn't know the Mississippi rules, and Maurice felt that someone should be with Bobo at all times.

For less than a minute he was in the store alone with Carolyn Bryant, the white woman working at the cash register. What he said, if anything, before I came in I don't know. While I was in the store, Bobo did nothing inappropriate. He didn't grab Mrs. Bryant, nor did he put his arms around her—that was the story she later told to the court. A counter separated the customers from the store clerk; Bobo would

have had to jump over it to get to Mrs. Bryant. Bobo didn't
ask her for a date or call her "baby." There was no lecherous
conversation between them. And after a few minutes he paid
for his items and we left the store together.

We had been outside the store only a few seconds when
Mrs. Bryant came out behind us, heading straight to her car.
As she walked, Bobo whistled at her. I think he wanted to get
a laugh out of us or something. He was always joking around,
and it was hard to tell when he was serious. It was a loud wolf
whistle, a big-city "whee wheeeee!" and it caught us all by
surprise. We all looked at each other, realizing that Bobo had
violated a longstanding unwritten law, a social taboo about
conduct between blacks and whites in the South. Suddenly
we felt we were in danger, and we stared at each other, all
with the same expression of fear and panic. Like a group of
boys who had thrown a rock through somebody's window,
we ran to the car. Bobo, with a slight limp from the polio
he'd contracted as a child, ran along with us, but not as panic-
stricken as we were. After seeing our fright, it did slowly
dawn on him that he had done something wrong.

In our rush to get away, someone dropped a lit cigarette
in the car. Maurice stopped and was determined to find the
smoldering cigarette before pulling out of Money. We all got
out and found it pretty quick, then jumped back into the car
and sped out of town just as fast as we could.

We were about two miles down the road when Maurice, in his rearview mirror, saw a car speeding behind us. He brought it to our attention, and we all thought that maybe we were being chased. Maurice hit the brakes and pulled over to the side of the road. Everybody got out and ran but me; the rest of them had a head start and I was afraid that I wouldn't be able to catch up with them or I would get separated from them. I scooted down in the backseat while they hurried off through the cotton field. The car soon passed by. It was only some neighbor on his way home. When the rest of them saw that nothing had happened, they got back into the car and we resumed our drive toward home.

"Please don't tell your father I whistled at that lady," Bobo pleaded. He was afraid that if my father found out about what he had done, he would be sent back to Chicago immediately. We didn't want that to happen so we promised to keep quiet for Bobo's sake. It never occurred to me that Bobo would be killed for whistling at a white woman. I thought he might be whipped if he were caught—but never murdered. If I had told Dad, he would have done one of two things: either he would have taken Bobo back to the store and made him apologize to Mrs. Bryant or he would have sent Bobo home as soon as possible. Either way, perhaps Bobo would be alive today.

It was dark now, and after Maurice dropped our neighbors off, he drove the rest of us home. We went to bed without saying anything at all about the incident. Bobo's indiscretion was our secret. At daybreak we were all up and ready for the cotton patch, having almost forgotten the events of the day before.

Later that evening, a girl who lived nearby told us she had heard about what happened in Money and that trouble was brewing. "I know the Bryants, and they are not going to forget what happened," she warned us. Her words renewed my panic. But all we did was to hope she wasn't right. Again I did not sense the true danger Bobo was in. So I kept silent.

On Friday nothing happened, so we forgot about the incident again. Our focus was now on our upcoming trip to Greenwood on Saturday. These trips were one of the bright moments in my life on the farm. Greenwood was about ten miles south of Money and about thirteen miles from our house. For us it was like Chicago's "Magnificent Mile." All of the farmworkers from the surrounding plantations would congregate in Greenwood on a Saturday night—the number of people you'd see was stunning.

My primary purpose there was to attend the movies. Of the three theaters in Greenwood, the two we usually went to were the Dixie Theater and the Walthall Theater. Both showed mostly westerns. If the money was right, I would go to both. But Maurice, Bobo, Wheeler, and our neighbor Roosevelt Crawford, known as Sunnyman, did not have time for a movie. They were looking for girls. So they went their own way into Greenwood. Fortunately, I was able to secure my own ride with Sunnyman's older brother, John Crawford. Robert chose not to join us, preferring to stay home to listen to his favorite radio program, *Gunsmoke.* The rest of us were excited about the trip.

Greenwood was the largest city in our county, Leflore. It was also the county seat. The most stunning things about the town were the lovely homes, stately mansions with well-manicured lawns. Even today, they are just as beautiful and immaculate as they were back in the 1950s. There was also the general splendor of the trip south via Money Road. Crossing the Yazoo River, we observed City Hall, an ornate white building where most of the town's business took place. On one of the corners was a statue in honor of the sons and daughters of the Confederacy. From here it was only a few minutes to Johnson Street, where all that we needed was within a few blocks.

Maurice, Bobo, Wheeler, and Sunnyman walked up and down Johnson Street, looking in the nightclubs and watching the people dance. From there they went over to the Blue Light Tavern on McLaurin Street. This was the violent section of Greenwood, a place that I stayed clear of. After spending a little time in the city, they went to the Four Fifths Plantation northwest of Greenwood, where there was a house party going on, with gambling and white lightning—homemade whiskey, 190 proof. They tasted the white lightning, but girls were not to be found.

I think I meanwhile saw a western about a lawman tracking down a bad guy, which I believe starred Randolph Scott. What I remember best about the movie was the lawman riding his horse with the rain pouring down, singing a song that went something like this: "Ole deacon got drunk and he stayed all day in his saddle to pray." I am sure the lawman caught his man. After the movies, I got some food—one of the treats we looked forward to was an ice-cream cone and fifty cents' worth of fish, or the famous foot-long hot dog. Then I, too, walked around on Johnson Street people-watching.

A night in Greenwood was exhausting. I always fell asleep during the ride home. We arrived home after midnight.

We had not been in bed two hours when we were startled awake.

According to Dad, he woke up after hearing a voice coming from the front porch. A man called out, "Preacher, Preacher." Upon hearing the voice, Dad said, he got up and went to see who was calling him. He asked, "Who is it?" and

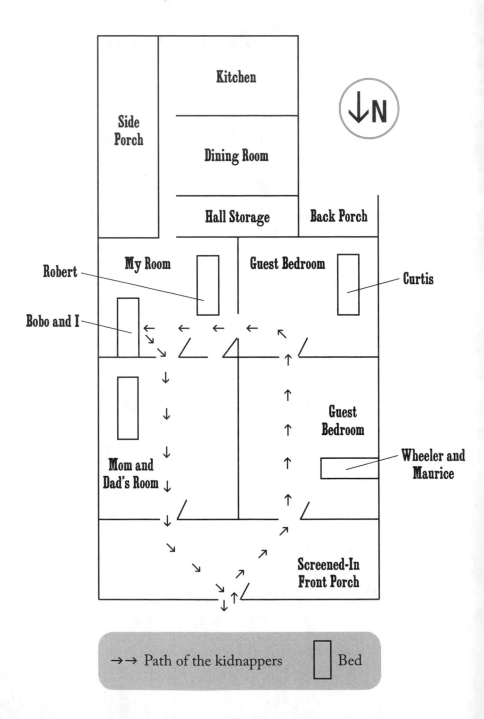

→→ Path of the kidnappers   ▯ Bed

the man responded, "This is Mr. Bryant. I want to talk to you and that boy."

When he opened the door, he saw two white men standing on the porch. One of them—J. W. Milam, we would learn later—was tall, thickset, and balding; he had a gun in one hand and a flashlight in the other. The second man was almost as tall but not as heavy; he was the one who had spoken, Roy Bryant. A third man stood behind Bryant, hiding his face from Dad. Dad believed he was a black man, someone who knew us.

The white men entered the house through our front guest room, where Wheeler and Maurice were sleeping. Dad woke Wheeler up first. Milam told Dad that Wheeler was not the boy he was looking for; he was looking for the fat boy from Chicago. Then I heard loud talking in my bedroom.

In my half-conscious state, I had no idea what was going on. Was I dreaming? Or was it a nightmare? Why were these white men in our bedroom at this hour? I rubbed my eyes and then shielded them, trying to see beyond the glare of the flashlight. The balding man ordered me to go back to sleep.

Dad had to shake Bobo for quite a while to wake him up. When he finally awoke, the balding man told Bobo to get up and put his clothes on. It was then that I realized they had come to take him away. It wasn't clear to me what was going on and why they wanted just him. At first I thought they had come to send him back to Chicago, but that didn't make sense at all.

I was lying there, frozen stiff and not moving, when my mother rushed into the room. She began pleading with the men not to take Bobo. I could hear the fear in her voice. She broke into a mixture of pleas and tears as she practically prayed for Bobo, asking the men not to harm him. The men ignored her, urging Bobo to hurry up and get dressed. He was still somewhat groggy and rubbing his eyes, but he quickly obeyed. My mother then offered them some money to not take Bobo away. I was now fully awake but still not moving. It was now crystal clear to me that these men were up to no good. They had come for Bobo, and no amount of begging, pleading, or payment was going to stop them. Although Dad had two shotguns in his closet, the 12-gauge and a .410, he never tried to get to them. If Dad had made a break for his guns, none of us would be alive today. I believe Milam and Bryant were prepared to kill us all at the slightest provocation. I am glad that Dad didn't do anything to put us all in danger.

Suddenly, the same panic I had felt after Bobo had whistled at Mrs. Bryant returned, and it was all I could do to stop trembling with fear, realizing that Bobo was not only in trouble but in grave danger. My fear soon escalated into terror, and I was still frozen stiff in my bed, unable to move or to say anything. My mother's pleas continued as the men pushed the now-dressed Bobo from the room. Bobo left that room without saying one word. There is no way I could have done that. Everyone along Dark Fear Road would have heard my screams.

At the time I didn't know what happened next, but according to my dad, the men took Bobo out to a car or truck that was waiting in the darkness. One of the men asked someone inside the vehicle if this was the right boy, and Dad said he heard a woman's voice respond that it was. Then the men drove off with Bobo, toward Money. Dad stood for a long while, he said, looking in that direction.

As for Mama, once the men were gone, she frantically ran next door to ask our white neighbors for help. When the man of the house, who was the straw boss of our farm, refused to offer any assistance, it only compounded my mother's hysteria. She was completely mortified at his refusal to help.

I must have stayed in the bed for hours, petrified. Wheeler and I were both awake, but we did not make a sound. Maurice, Robert, and my nephew Curtis, who had just come to stay with us that night after spending the week with his aunt, slept through the whole ordeal. There was nothing the rest of us could do but to wait and pray that Bobo was going to be all right. For a long time we were all quiet together, hoping that the men had only come to frighten Bobo and that he would soon be brought back to the house. Each time I heard a car on the road, I waited to see if it was the men bringing him back. The only thing that penetrated the silence was my mother's voice, choked with fear. She could not be consoled.

"I am not going to stay in this house another night," my mother told Daddy. In order to calm her down, he agreed to take her to her brother's house for safety. My mother's brother Crosby Smith lived in Sumner, which was about twenty-five miles north of Money. (This is the same little town that my mother's parents had moved to in the early 1900s.) After my mother left our house on Dark Fear Road, she never set foot in it again.

After taking Mom to Uncle Crosby's house, Daddy drove with Uncle Crosby around Money, looking for the men and Bobo. Then, as the sun came up on the morning of August 28, Dad went to the home of Elbert Parker, Wheeler's uncle, to make arrangements to get Wheeler out of Mississippi. Dad knew that Mr. Elbert had another brother who lived in Duck Hill, Mississippi, which was fifteen miles from Winona, the location of the nearest train station. Dad and Mr. Elbert took Wheeler to William Parker's home for safety and to see to it that Wheeler got on the next train headed for Chicago.

I talked with Mr. William in June 2008, five months before he died at 105 years of age, about what had happened that day when Dad showed up with Wheeler. He said he told Dad that Duck Hill was no safer than Money—"the whites were killing blacks out there too." Nevertheless he promised that he would see to Wheeler getting home safely. He said that he had never seen anyone as scared as Wheeler was. What made matters worse for Wheeler was that he had missed the week's last scheduled train to Chicago and had to wait until Monday to leave Mississippi.

When Maurice, Robert, and Curtis awoke and learned what had happened to Bobo, they shook their heads in shock and horror. But all we could do while Daddy was gone was to continue to wait and hope.

After Daddy came back from Duck Hill, he notified George Smith, sheriff of Leflore County, who sent his deputy out to take our statement about Bobo's abduction. Then it was time to make that dreaded call to Bobo's mother. Daddy felt we could wait no longer, so he sent Curtis up to the boss man's house to use the phone. Curtis called his mother in Chicago, and she relayed his message to Bobo's mother and grandmother.

After the deputy sheriff came, it seemed like everybody in the county knew about Bobo's abduction. Neighbors from all around Money came to visit us, and these visits from friends and neighbors were just what we needed during this very sad time. Many of them offered to help, asking if there was anything they could do to make our lives easier. They provided comfort and food, and we deeply appreciated their help.

Curtis stayed around until that evening but then returned to his aunt's house in Greenwood. In a matter of hours, four people I had spent time with were no longer at the house. Three of them—Mom, Curtis, and Wheeler—had left the house willingly, and the other, Bobo, was snatched against his will.

August 28, 1955, had been the longest day of my life. It was the first day there was no laughter in our house. And I believe that unless you can laugh and hear laughter there, a house isn't a home.

Dad also feared that the house was no longer safe for us, so he sent Robert and me to stay with neighbors, Mr. Clint Lewis and his wife, Gertrude. They owned their property deep in the woods and had one son and a niece living with them. We spent three nights—Sunday, Monday, and Tuesday—with the Lewis family. Living with them, however, didn't mean we were freed from working in the cotton fields. That Monday, like clockwork, we were back in the fields, picking the cotton. All the while I was working the fields, my mind never left Bobo, and I was wondering where he was and if he was all right. The hardest part was not knowing what had happened to him.

By Monday, Sheriff Smith had arrested Roy Bryant and his half brother J. W. Milam and charged them with kidnapping. But there was no news that day or the next about Bobo's whereabouts.

On Wednesday, around noon, the deputy sheriff came out to the cotton fields and talked to my father. Dad didn't say anything to us but very quietly left the fields with the deputy. I knew something had happened; I had a feeling then that they had found Bobo. The question in my mind was whether he was alive or dead. The deep sorrow I felt told me the answer.

Dad asked our neighbor John Crawford to drive him up to Sumner. He came back that evening with the grim news that Bobo had been found floating in the Tallahatchie River about twenty miles north of where we lived, near the town of Philipp in Tallahatchie County. Dad had seen and identified Bobo.

It was devastating news to my family and me. My soul was hurt and my appetite left me again. The day after Bobo's kidnapping I hadn't eaten at all. I don't know how much weight I lost, but my sister Hallie lost ten pounds in ten days. My sister Thelma lost her appetite too, for both food and drink; she would take one bite and then feel full instantly. We were unable to contain our grief. For the first time in my life, I thought about shooting a gun at another person. I had

Milam in mind—I didn't know his name yet, but I remembered his face.

Dad sat on the front-porch swing, quietly contemplating what he would do next. He would sigh and utter only grunts—*ugh, ugh*. Mom was no longer there to console him or to help him understand what had happened. Dad had gone to see Mom at Uncle Crosby's house after identifying Bobo's body. They had decided that for her own safety and peace of mind, Mom should leave Mississippi for Chicago.

Tallahatchie County sheriff H. C. Strider and officials from that county insisted that Dad bury Bobo's body without delay. The undertaker told Dad that the body had to be buried quickly because it was in such bad shape. I never did see Bobo's body. But I did see a picture later, and it was the most grotesque, disfigured image of a human being I had ever seen. That image has lived with me to this day.

Dad told them that there was a little church nearby with a cemetery where Bobo could be buried—East Money Church of God in Christ, where he had been the pastor. The same day Bobo's body was found, Uncle Crosby followed the hearse out to the cemetery. Two young men—Buck Jones, who also lived on Mr. Frederick's plantation, and J. T. Lewis, Gertrude and Clint Lewis's son—dug the grave. We were told to get ready for the funeral, so we left the field, got dressed, and piled into the little Ford sedan with Maurice behind the wheel. The funeral home had made all the arrangements to get Bobo's remains to the gravesite. His body was encased in a wooden box next to the grave.

Before the service started, Uncle Crosby told Dad that he didn't think that Bobo's grandmother, Aunt Alma, would want him buried in Mississippi. In fact, he told Dad that Bobo's body would be buried in Chicago. Then the sheriff of Leflore County showed up, driving a 1955 Ford, and stopped the proceedings. Sheriff Smith told the undertaker that Bobo would not be buried in Mississippi and ordered him to take Bobo's body back to Greenwood and prepare it to be shipped to Chicago. The undertaker told Sheriff Smith that he had instructions from Tallahatchie County to bury Bobo's body immediately. Sheriff Smith let the undertaker know that he was sheriff of Leflore County and the undertaker was to do what he said. Sheriff Smith got in his car and sped off, spinning his wheels and throwing gravel in our direction.

We learned later that Aunt Alma and Bobo's mother, Mamie Till Bradley, had asked Mayor Richard J. Daley of Chicago and Governor William Stratton of Illinois to intercede for them to get Bobo's body returned to Chicago. Uncle Crosby and my mother accompanied the body there. Mom never set foot in Mississippi again.

The next day, the rest of us were back in the cotton fields. But our home quickly became a focal point for journalists

and the NAACP. Folks from nearby and across the country arrived at the house to talk about politics and other civil
rights issues. Of course, Bobo's murder was the main topic of
discussion. Dad later said that the NAACP was calling it a
lynching, but I remember that Dad often referred to it as a
"slaying." I had heard of someone being lynched, but *slaying*
was a new word for me. Somehow there seemed to me to
be a vast difference between a murder and a slaying. To me,
slaying was something committed by a gang of men, a gang
that hunts you down like you were a wild animal and without
mercy or reason takes your life.

In my mind, what happened to Bobo was indeed worse
than murder, and I felt that surely something would be done
about it. There was a hue and cry from all over the nation, and
newspaper after newspaper condemned the vicious killing.
Even in Mississippi, many state and local officials denounced
the crime. While Governor Hugh White refused to define
Bobo's murder as a lynching, he labeled it a straight-out murder, called for a full investigation, and said that the state of
Mississippi deplored such conduct on the part of its citizens.
These reactions gave me hope that justice would be served
and that the murderers would pay for their crime.

5

The Trial

THE NEXT COUPLE OF WEEKS were busy, especially for Dad. By this time, Robert and I had returned from staying with the Lewises, and not a day went by when we weren't visited by somebody. Civil rights activists, well-wishers, newspaper reporters, and photographers would come to the cotton fields to interview Dad and to take pictures. Even a television crew came out one day. This was the first time I had ever seen a television camera. All of this attention helped us get through those dark days without Bobo.

About a week after Bobo's body was discovered, we received a different kind of visitor. An official from Tallahatchie County came to our home with papers saying that we were to report to Sumner to give depositions in the case. (I didn't know what a "deposition" was; I just knew that we had to go up to Sumner and talk to the lawyers there.) After presenting the summonses, the man pulled out a ring that had been found on the body and asked Dad if he recognized it. I spoke up: "That's Bobo's ring."

I also remember one day when members of the NAACP came to the house, including the state's field representative, Medgar Evers. It was Medgar's task to round up prosecution witnesses for the upcoming trial, and he didn't have too much time to get it done. Also working to find and secure witnesses was Dr. T. R. M. Howard, a beloved African American physician from historic Mound Bayou, Mississippi, a town populated and governed entirely by blacks. We were so proud of Dr. Howard, who would not be intimidated by whites or the Klan.

It was through the tireless efforts of Dr. Howard and Medgar Evers that Mamie was prepared to testify about identifying her son's body, and a surprise witness to the crime itself was located. An eighteen-year-old black man named Willie Reed said that he had heard screams coming from a barn on a plantation managed by J. W. Milam's brother Leslie. Then, Reed said, he was accosted by J. W. Milam, who asked him if had heard or seen anything; he had enough sense not to let on at the time how much he had witnessed.

Medgar and Dad had a long conversation, and I later learned that Medgar had congratulated Dad for his courage in agreeing to testify—prosecutors needed him to identify Bryant and Milam as the men who took Bobo. Medgar stressed that Dad should work to retain as much of his memory of what had happened as possible and speak only the truth.

Milam had threatened my dad on the night of the abduction, telling him that if he said anything at all to incriminate them, he would never live to see his next birthday. Our neighbors were warning Dad to be careful, and many people sent telegrams urging him to leave the state. But he was determined to stay and to fight. He said it wasn't something he chose to do, but something he felt he had to do.

When I myself was subpoenaed to be a witness at the trial, I must admit that I was a little bit nervous. But I saw the courage my father was displaying, and it was all the encouragement I needed—if he wasn't afraid, then I wasn't either. Even at this early age, it was my belief that if we had to go down, then we would go down fighting.

Roy Bryant and J. W. Milam's murder trial began on Monday, September 19, a little less than three weeks after Bobo's body was dredged from the river. They were being tried up in Tallahatchie County, where the body was found;

our neighbor John Crawford fearlessly agreed to drive us to the courthouse in Sumner every day. We'd leave for court around eight in the morning and get there by nine.

After we got to the old brick courthouse, I was escorted to a witness room at the back of the courtroom, where I was told to wait to be called. There were no sheriff's deputies there to protect us, but that was no surprise to Dad. On the first day, Maurice and Robert were there in the witness room with me, but they had to go back to the cotton field, so they couldn't stay. Most of the time I was alone, although sometimes my father or other witnesses were there with me. From the room, I could vaguely hear what was going on in the trial. At one time I heard Medgar Evers's name called but I wasn't sure why; it may have been when the court's clerk was merely noting the people slated to testify in the case.

While I was not able to actually watch much of the trial, during the recess or when they took breaks, I was allowed to go outside the courthouse and see all the people milling around on the courthouse lawn. There were hundreds there, as though the state fair were about to open. Recesses were also my chance to escape the heat and humidity of the courtroom—the overhead fans provided very little relief, especially in the witness room where I was. I might go to the nearby store to buy a pop or a candy bar. There were no restaurants where a black person could buy lunch.

Upon entering the courtroom again after recess, I could see Bryant and Milam on the far side with their wives and children, including Carolyn Bryant. They seemed to be having a good time, laughing and talking with friends and relatives who had come to give them moral support. As my eyes quickly scanned the crowd, I also noticed the Tallahatchie County sheriff, H. C. Strider, who at nearly three hundred pounds was pretty hard to miss. Everybody knew the sheriff was a big landowner with a large number of black sharecroppers—and airplanes that flew over the cotton fields dusting them with chemicals. It was his duty to search everybody as they entered the courtroom. I don't think any of the white people were searched, just the blacks. There were reports that he had received a lot of threatening letters, so I guess he wasn't taking any chances.

Like everything else in Mississippi at that time, it was a segregated courtroom. White men occupied most of the hundred or so seats. What black spectators there were—and there must have been forty or fifty—were confined to the back of the courtroom. The reporters there covering the trial were also separated by race. They were instructed by Judge Curtis Swango that there were to be no pictures taken during the trial, so they were to get all their pictures before the session began.

Most of what occurred in the courtroom during the five-day trial was told to me by Dad later in the evenings as we drove home with Mr. Crawford. Nothing much happened on the first day; from what I could gather, most of the time was given to selecting the jury. More than one hundred potential jurors were called before they decided on ten white men; two more white men would be selected on Tuesday. One of the reasons it took so long, Dad told me, was that so many of the potential jurors had contributed money for the defense, and some of them were relatives of the defense lawyers. I was curious to know if any of them were related to the prosecutors, Gerald Chatham and Robert B. Smith III.

If convicted of murder, Bryant and Milam faced life in prison—the death penalty was never mentioned, much to Dad's disgust. But the defense was doing all it could to argue the body taken from the river was not Bobo. No autopsy had been conducted to confirm his identity—I never knew exactly why—and while Bryant and Milam admitted to abducting him, they insisted they had not harmed him. They claimed they had let him go after Mrs. Bryant said he wasn't the one who had insulted her that day. They were not only murderers, they were lying wonders. Some of their supporters went so far as to claim that the NAACP had planted the body to further its own agenda.

So Chatham and Smith had to show that what the defense was saying was untrue. That was the main reason I had been called as a witness—to confirm that the ring that was found on the body was Bobo's. The prosecutors were not interested in what happened at the store or our encounter with Carolyn Bryant. I found it odd that they didn't ask me about that.

As it turned out, I never took the stand to testify, because they focused on Mamie's testimony instead. I think she arrived on the second day of the trial, accompanied by her father, John Carthan; Rayfield Moody, her cousin and a union leader in Chicago; and Charles Diggs, an African American congressman from the state of Michigan. There was a lot of commotion when Mamie entered the courtroom. Breaking all protocol, the photographers rushed to take her picture, and reporters both black and white swarmed around her, asking her questions about her son and what she hoped to add to the trial proceedings.

After things quieted down, I stood before the judge with Mamie and the other witnesses who had been called to identify Bobo's body. He reassured us that we would be treated fairly and that the sheriff's department of Tallahatchie County would protect us. Looking back, I know that we had no protection but the mercy of God. If somebody had tried to harm us, I don't think the sheriff would have done anything to prevent it. At the time, though, I somehow believed what the judge was saying.

Even so, I was a little nervous with so many white people crowding around us, staring at us, but never saying anything to us. The judge, the jury, the lawyers, the audience—just about everyone was white. Medgar Evers was in and out of the trial, though, and I remember seeing Congressman Diggs, sweltering in the hot and humid courtroom with the rest of us. And despite my apprehension, I was certain that Bryant and Milam were going to be convicted, since there were eyewitnesses who had pointed them out—including my father.

I will never forget that Wednesday, the third day of the trial, because that was the day Dad took the stand as the state's first witness. He was on the witness stand for about half an hour. There were the usual questions. District Attorney Chatham asked Dad to state his name and where he lived. He asked Dad where Money was in relation to the town of Philipp (where Bobo's body was found), and how long he had lived there. Whose place did he live on? What kind of house did he live in? How many rooms? Dad was then asked to describe the layout of the house. He was asked about the night of the abduction. Who was in the house with him? Did one or more person visit his home that night, and if they did, at what time? Dad answered in a booming voice, letting the court know that he wasn't intimidated, he wasn't afraid.

Dad described how the kidnappers had come to the front door at around 2 A.M. and how Bryant had introduced himself. Then the DA asked Dad to point out the other man with Bryant that night, if he saw him in the courtroom. Dad stood up, pointed to Milam, and said, "There he is."

The photographers couldn't resist taking pictures. I've seen those photos of Dad so many times, with his finger pointed at the accused, that I forget that I was in the witness room and not in the courtroom. Dad later said that while the few blacks in the courtroom were in agreement with him, the whites stared at him. He said that he stared back. From the looks on their faces, Dad knew that he had to leave Mississippi.

It was the first time in the history of the state, we were told later, that a black man had stood up in a courtroom and accused a white man of anything. Riding back home with him later that day, I felt extremely proud.

One night soon after Dad testified, we boys were staying with neighbors and Dad was at home all alone. He went to bed, he told us, but could not sleep. He was so restless he decided to spend the night at his church. While there, he said, a spirit of fear came over him. That helped him to make up his mind that when the trial was over, it would be time to go. Another factor that helped him make the decision to move was that he knew Mama wasn't coming back. She was completely devastated by what had happened to Bobo, and I don't think she ever got over it—none of us did.

Every day of the trial was important to us, but many people feel that the fourth day was especially crucial. The courtroom was as packed as ever as Mamie took the stand. With tears in her eyes, she told the court how she identified her son's body in Chicago at A. A. Rayner & Sons Funeral Home, where it had been sent for burial.

I had been unable to attend the funeral—no one from Mississippi had gone—but we heard about it from my sister Hallie. She said it was a very sad affair and that she did all she could do to keep from fainting. A lot of people just keeled over after viewing Bobo's disfigured remains in the open casket.

After Mamie stepped down, the prosecution called surprise witness Willie Reed. He testified to what he had seen on the day Bobo was abducted—J. W. Milam leaving the barn where Reed had heard screams. Under questioning by prosecutor Robert Smith, Reed also reported that earlier, when he was on his way to the store, he had seen a green and white truck pass him, with four white men in the cab and three black men in the back, one of them sitting down in the truck bed. Reed testified that the seated person resembled the picture of Emmett Till that he later saw in the paper. After a few more witnesses, the state rested its case.

The first witness for the defense was Carolyn Bryant. She had been at the trial every day, but now she was on the stand to recall what had happened in town the Wednesday before the abduction. The prosecution objected that her story was not relevant to the case, and Judge Swango agreed, so she wasn't allowed to testify in front of the jury. But the judge let her tell her story for the record without the jury being present—and without being under oath. So she couldn't be cross-examined, and if she lied, she couldn't be charged with perjury. She told the court that Bobo had grabbed her and spoken lasciviously to her, but as I mentioned, he was alone with her for less than a minute, there was a counter separating them, and he did nothing inappropriate while I was with him in the store.

We all were in the courtroom on Friday morning for the final day of the trial, as the state and the defense delivered their closing arguments. The defense dwelled on two claims by their "expert" witnesses: that because the body was so badly decomposed, it could not be identified as Bobo's, and that it had to have been in the river ten to fifteen days—more than the three Bobo had been missing. (These same witnesses had been forced to admit on cross-examination that a body might decompose faster if it had been badly beaten.)

The prosecution's response to these arguments was powerful and widely circulated. Mr. Chatham remembered a day when his son had come to him and told him, "Dad, I've found old Shep," his dead dog. His son took him by the hand and led him to a ravine where the dog's badly decomposed body was rotting in the sun. "That dog's body was rotting and the meat was falling off of its bone," Chatham told a packed courthouse, "but my little boy pointed to it and said, 'That's old Shep, Pa. That's old Shep.'"

Chatham said that his son did not need an undertaker to identify his dog, and Mamie didn't need one to identify Bobo. "All we need is someone who loved and cared for him," he said. "If there was one ear left, one hairline, one part of his nose, any part of Emmett Till's body, then I say to you that Mamie Bradley was God's given witness to identify him."

Mr. Chatham did a marvelous job throughout the state's summation, telling stories with such passion that it brought tears to listeners' eyes. We all agreed with Mamie that he had done about all he could to prosecute the two men.

Mamie and her group left the courtroom before the verdict came in. At the time I had no idea why. But now I know that she could tell what the result would be from the looks on the whites' faces. Dad and I stayed in the courthouse. All the segregationists in the state of Mississippi were not going to keep us from hearing the verdict. It took the jury a little over an hour to decide Bryant and Milam's fate: not guilty.

We were stunned and left with a sense of hopelessness that there was no justice for a black man in Mississippi if the case had anything to do with a white person. Dad said that no matter what he said or did, the white jurors were going to free those men. His testimony, an eyewitness account of the kidnapping, meant nothing to them. Dad said that he had heard it said that a black man's life meant nothing in Mississippi. Now he knew what they said was true. He had tasted firsthand the plight of the black man. What he saw crushed him.

As for me, I was enraged and embittered by the verdict. I saw for the first time the evil that was in the heart of the segregationists. Even after fifty years, prejudice of the whites of Mississippi against the blacks is still baffling to me. Some things in the world have changed for the better, but far too many of these inequities remain. Needless to say, the death of Bobo and the acquittal of his murderers left a hole in my heart.

What made it worse were the shouts of victory, glee, and sheer joy coming from the whites inside and outside of the courtroom. Bryant and Milam lit up cigars; folks hugged them and slapped them on the back. Even Sheriff Strider was pleased with the verdict. As we were walking to our car, we could only look back at them all, realizing that even after this brutal murder we were still alone. There was no one to help us. Even the whites who were incensed by the murder did nothing. They didn't want to get involved. I felt defeated, not by Milam and Bryant, but by the justice system of Mississippi.

6

Fear and Flight

WHEN WE ARRIVED HOME after the not guilty verdict came in, Daddy went to feed his hogs and gather his thoughts. That evening, he gathered us together and said, "Boys, we can't stay here any longer." They were the sweetest words I had ever heard him say.

We started packing our things, some to sell and some to give away. No white folks came around after the trial, not even the boss man, Mr. Frederick. He was a good, decent man, but I think he was frightened.

The house belonged to Mr. Frederick, so we didn't need to sell it, but we did have to get rid of a brand-new stove and refrigerator, which we returned to the store. In our hurry to get out of Mississippi, we left a lot of things behind, including our dog, Dallas. To this day I don't know why we left Dallas instead of taking him with us. Maybe Dad thought that dogs were not allowed on the train. All I know is that it added to my sorrow.

We also left many of the newspaper clippings about the trial. (It seems that for a while the news of the trial was everywhere. I know it was in the Chicago papers, particularly the *Chicago Defender*, the black weekly, which had sent reporters to cover the trial.) We even left the letters from people all over the world—Russia, Japan, France—expressing their dismay at the murder. I wish we had saved these documents, to keep a paper trail, so to speak, but we had no idea that over half a century later people would still be talking about Bobo and his murder.

The following Monday, we would drive out to the house of my dad's brother, Uncle Will, in Browning, and from there to Winona to get the train. I must admit I left with mixed emotions. The house on Dark Fear Road was the only home I had ever really known, so there were a lot of pleasant memories. But my last impression was that this refuge was not secure enough to protect me from evil men who planned murder. Even my bedroom was not a safe haven, because killers had walked into it and snatched Bobo from us.

Once we left our house, I learned later, one of Mr. Frederick's nephews and his wife remodeled it. But sixteen years later, in 1971, a tornado swept through the region and destroyed it, killing the two occupants.

As we drove through the town of Money for the last time, I took a final look at the street and the store where the tragedy had begun. Even now, more than fifty years later, I can still visualize the main street with its few stores and buildings.

The cotton gin was the first building we passed. You could hear the loud noise of the vacuum pumps. Next was the post office, with Dr. Shelly's office adjacent to it. Dr. Shelly waited on both black and white patients—blacks could go to his office on Wednesday evenings only. We passed Mr. Wolf's store, the place where Bobo bought his fireworks. The next store was Mr. Chatham's, where you could buy a pop for a dime.

Mr. Roberts's store followed. The Robertses were a white family who had raised Ted Griffins, a black boy who became a basketball star at Money Vocational High School. Mr. Roberts had also experienced the wrath of Roy Bryant. One Wednesday evening he did not close his store, which was a rule the other shopkeepers in Money had decided on to give themselves the afternoon off. Roy Bryant went to Mr. Roberts's store, gun in hand, and made him close down.

As we passed Bryant's store, which was separated from Mr. Roberts's store by a street, I did not see anyone in or outside it. The last store was Mr. Ben Roy's. It was the only gas station in the city of Money. He was very decent to the blacks, but his wife, well, that's another story. So there were a total of five stores in Money.

A couple of blocks down Money Road, we passed a turn road that took drivers across the Illinois Central Railroad tracks. On one side of that road sat Money Vocational Grade and High School, the campus for black students in grades one through twelve. On the other side sat a little cafe, the last business establishment in the city.

Within an hour we were at my uncle Will's house, where we made the final preparations to leave Mississippi. Aunt Leah made us a big lunch, which we took with us to the train station in Winona.

Dad left his car with Uncle Will, and we boarded the train to Chicago. One thing that sticks in my mind is Aunt Leah's lunch. It was one of the best I had ever had, because it was the first time I had ever eaten tuna fish. I don't remember exactly how long the train ride took, but I know I was glad to be going to the city where Bobo had lived, and I couldn't wait to see all the things he had told me about.

We arrived in Chicago that same day. We were met at the Twelfth Street Station by my older brothers James and Cornelius, my sisters Willie Mae and Hallie, and my mother, whom I hadn't seen in thirty days. With my mother there with me, I felt safe again. The family was once more united.

We moved into a four-family flat in Argo, not too far from Chicago. We lived upstairs and Hallie's family—including Wheeler—lived downstairs. James and Cornelius owned the building. Mamie was living on the South Side of Chicago at the time, so I would only get a chance to see her at family gatherings.

Me with Wheeler Parker Jr., shortly after we moved to Argo.

The next day I was awakened by the rain. The kids in the neighborhood were all in school. Unlike in Mississippi, the school year had already started. My own first day of school was awkward, to say the least. I went from being in the top five in my class in Mississippi to being only a little boy from the South, shy beyond measure, unfamiliar to all but my niece Elaine, Wheeler's sister. The kids were very sympathetic to me, though, very much aware of the tragic things that had happened to me.

The school I attended, Argo Elementary, was all black, and so was our neighborhood. In the Chicago area, blacks were not segregated by law, but they were still segregated. Whites would refuse to sell homes in white neighborhoods to black people, or they would use intimidation and violence to keep blacks from moving in. In Argo, no blacks lived outside the town's two black neighborhoods: south of Sixty-Third Street between Seventy-Sixth Avenue on the west and Harlem Avenue on the east, where we lived, and west of Archer Road, home to the blacks who lived "'cross town."

After we were settled, Daddy spent about three months traveling around the northwestern United States with the NAACP, talking about the trial and what had happened to Bobo. The NAACP leadership was very upset by the verdict; they felt it was a total miscarriage of justice, and so did Dad. These were some of the things he stressed during the speaking tour with the organization. Later, he was presented the John Russwurm Award for his speaking (Russwurm was famous for starting the first black newspaper in America). Besides Daddy, the family hardly ever talked about the trial, the verdict, or Bobo's death.

Dad, who had honed his skills as a farmer, had to start all over again at the age of sixty-three. For him it was like working on a job for forty-seven years and being suddenly laid off without compensation. Of course, the many factories around

Argo would not hire him because of his age. For a while, with Bobo's murder still fresh in the news, he helped the NAACP raise a lot of money, as did Mamie. But for all their hard work and success on the organization's behalf, Dad and Mamie received little compensation. After the speaking tour ended, Dad got a job as a custodian, cleaning up at a night-club. He didn't make very much money, but he was thrifty, so it was just enough for us to get by.

Making the adjustment to city living was not easy for any of us. It seemed like the people we'd known in Mississippi were more neighborly than those we met in the Chicago area. On the farm, we helped each other more and did not expect to be paid for our services. In Argo people expected to be compensated for even going to the store for you. Even now, when I do things for my neighbors, I do them because they are neighbors, and not for money.

In other ways, too, the things we had taken for granted on the farm were no longer there for us. Buying eggs, chick-ens, fish, milk, and fresh vegetables was unheard of in the South. Now that we were living in the city, we had to buy our food. But these were small disadvantages. There were so many other things that made life much easier in the city.

For example, we no longer needed a car. Down in Mississippi, everything was so far away you needed a car or a horse and wagon to get around. Now, even my school was just across the street from where I lived. Riding a bus was another new experience for us; if we needed to go to Chicago, the CTA bus stop was only two blocks away. In fact, Dad never bought another car.

But for me, the most mind-boggling change was to my own daily routine. I went from working in the cotton fields ten hours a day to not working at all for the first two years. The only thing I had to do was to go to school. After school I had to fill up the coal bucket, do my homework, and watch Mickey Mouse on TV. Slowly it dawned on me that compared with living on the cotton farm, living in the North was a dream. If someone had told me that such a life existed, I would not have believed them. The only things I really missed were the fishing and rabbit hunting.

Then there was the abrupt change in the weather. In the winter, Chicago was cold but beautiful to me. The below-zero temperatures were brutal, but the snowfall made up for it. As kids in Mississippi, we had longed for snow; I remember it snowing only two times while I lived there. Now it snowed five or six times a month. Even now I love to see it snow. The one drawback I can remember is that I only had a thin coat. I had to hurry up and get the proper clothes to do battle with "the almighty hawk, Mr. Wind," which Lou Rawls sang about with so much passion. Believe it or not, I was ice-skating before the first winter was over.

Is it possible to have twelve years' worth of fun in one year? If it's not possible, I came close in that first year. The fun made the adjustment to Chicago's winter much easier. But it wasn't enough for me to overcome the tragedy of Bobo's death. The hole was still in my heart.

One event in particular reminded us of the injustice we were trying so hard to escape. Soon after we moved north, a grand jury convened in Leflore County to decide whether Roy Bryant and J. W. Milam would be tried for Bobo's kidnapping. If tried and convicted, they each faced a maximum sentence of ten years in prison. Sheriff George Smith of Leflore County promised Dad that things would be different at the second trial, and he asked him if he would return to testify. Dad held out hope that something would be done to these men, so when he was summoned, he returned to Mississippi in November 1955. But again he was bitterly disappointed, when he learned that the grand jury of Leflore County was no different from the jury of Tallahatchie County. Even though Milam and Bryant had confessed that they took Bobo, the grand jury refused to indict them. They were not about to allow a white man to be prosecuted for killing a black person. There would not be a kidnapping trial.

For us, it was like rubbing salt in a raw, open wound. I think after that we made up our minds to try to put the whole affair behind us or else the disgust would be too much of a burden on our future. Missing Bobo, and remembering what had happened to him, I was determined to make something of my life and not to become the victim of bullies or anyone else who might try to hurt me.

7

In Argo

IN SPITE OF THE IMMEDIATE IMPROVEMENT in my living conditions, the horrors of Bobo's death were still with me. I couldn't shake the many thoughts of him. What if we had stayed home that night? What if we had told Dad? What did Carolyn Bryant tell her husband? Why were these men so evil?

The teachers and kids at Argo Elementary helped me to get through the heartbreak and sorrow that I felt. My sixth-grade classmates treated me like I had been there all along. I was no stranger to them, and this meant a lot to me. The little things they did for me made my new surroundings easier to adjust to. For example, during the physical exercise period, the two biggest boys in the sixth grade had the honor of selecting teammates for a quick basketball game. Charles L. Manning, who was the unofficial class leader, selected me third to play on his team. His confidence in me was a great boost to my morale. Because of simple little things like this, my heart was healing, slowly but surely. All thirty-four kids in that class are still on good terms.

Mr. Charles Ploszek, my sixth-grade teacher and the principal of the school, was great. He was white, short, and stocky, with a huge smile. There I was, a young black boy fresh out of Mississippi, looking at a white teacher for the first time in my life. What a surprise! (In fact, all the teachers, except Mrs. Simonton, were white.) Mr. Ploszek welcomed me to his classroom with much kindness and understanding. For a few days he paid special attention to me, until he found out that I could do the work he assigned to me. He did two other things that stayed with me. First, he made me part of the milk boys' team. Our job was to meet the milk truck and fill the milk order for each classroom. Then, after Christmas break, he made me a patrol boy. Patrol boys were crossing guards with certain privileges, such as getting out of class early at lunch time and when school was over for the day.

The fifth-grade teacher, Mr. Irwin Alvin Gnippe, was the kindest of them all. I didn't know at the time that he was Jewish; he was just another white man to me. He came to me one day to talk about the ordeal I had been through. I later thought that perhaps because he was Jewish, he could identify with the pain I had suffered in Mississippi, since I had been told how much Jewish people had suffered too. I could sense his concern and could see the disgust in his eyes. If I had any apprehensions about being around white teachers, they disappeared around him. There wasn't a prejudiced vein in his body—the world needs more people like that. To think of him is like a breath of fresh air.

Through the kindness and acceptance of both teachers and students, I was soon able to focus on my new surroundings and not on Bobo's murder. The help that I had been looking for in Mississippi, I found in this little school right across the street from my new home. With the help of William, Wheeler's younger brother, I was introduced to new friends. The tragedy began to fade into a distant yesterday.

As the years passed, I began taking on more responsibilities again. I got a job delivering the *Chicago Sun-Times* for about a year and a half, and then I got a shoeshine box and started shining shoes in the streets in and around Argo—I think I charged twenty cents. Later I got my first real job setting pins at a bowling alley. Shining shoes in the streets prepared me later for shining shoes in Wheeler's barber shop, which was also in Argo. Wheeler had started cutting hair when he was about seventeen, experimenting on me and his brother even before he went to barber school.

My ninth-grade class photo.

After sixth grade, I attended an integrated middle school and high school. During the school day, black and white students attended class together, played sports together, even ate together in the little cafe across the street from the school. But after school, blacks and whites had limited contact. In fact, the whites acted like they didn't know us.

After graduating from high school in 1962, I worked at Dearborn Glass in Argo, and then at Reynolds Metals Company in McCook, Illinois, where I went through their apprenticeship program and became a pipe fitter, the occupation I would remain in for the rest of my working life. (Pipe fitters install the pipes, pumps, and valves used in heating and cooling and other systems.) In 1964 I met Annie Cole, my future wife. She is from La Grange, Illinois, a graduate of Lyons Township High School. We were married on June 12, 1971. We are still together and madly in love.

In 1966, Dr. Martin Luther King Jr. came to Chicago to expand the civil rights movement. Practically every day there was something in the paper or on the nightly news about Dr. King and his campaign.

The organizers told us it was a nonviolent movement and that if you were a part of it, you couldn't retaliate if attacked. Even if they spat on you, you were not to do anything but take it. While I sincerely believed in Dr. King's goals, I didn't agree with his nonviolent strategy at the time—if somebody hit me, I was going to hit him back. I remember being simply amazed to see footage on television of black people being pulled from their cars and beaten during civil rights marches. The victims were not even part of the marches—they just happened to be black and passing through the area on their way home. I would have run over every one of those whites before I allowed them to pull me from my car. The white killers taking Bobo out of bed had left me determined to defend myself.

I knew that the tactics Dr. King used in the South were not going to get the same reaction from northern residents, particularly in Chicago, with its history of racist hostility. There was talk then about Birmingham, Alabama, being the most segregated city in America, but I was willing to bet that Chicago was right up there with it. Like me, other black Chicagoans were reluctant to embrace Dr. King's calls for passive resistance. He should have anticipated this reaction from the very first speeches he gave. For the first time in his life he was soundly booed by some of the young black men from our neighborhoods. They wanted to fight back.

In the early part of July, a major riot erupted in the black neighborhoods of Chicago's West Side, leading to widespread destruction and two deaths. Dr. King was clearly discouraged by the outbreak and the later presence of the National Guard to quell the disturbance. He blamed civic leadership and the city's intolerable conditions for the riot, while the leaders pointed to him as the instigator. Now Dr. King's movement had to fight another enemy as the press zeroed in on him, holding him partly responsible for fomenting bad feelings among "normally well-behaved" residents. Nevertheless, Dr. King and his cohorts persisted in their struggle to make Chicago an open and just city; he promised to soldier on, "not to turn back."

But there was more trouble ahead. During a demonstration for open housing in Marquette Park, Dr. King and his forces were greeted by an angry mob of whites hurling bottles and bricks. Even Dr. King had to remark that the attacks they endured on Chicago's Southwest Side far exceeded the opposition he had faced in Mississippi, Georgia, and Alabama.

Like most of us, Dr. King learned a vital lesson about the civil rights movement in Chicago, and it would serve him well during the last two years of his brief but brilliant life.

In one way I felt vindicated—I knew my instincts about his tactics were right—but in another way I was saddened by his failure to accomplish his mission. His failure belonged to all of us. In later years I would come to realize that Dr. King's nonviolent approach was the right way to go. You can't defeat racism through violence, but you can through the courts.

As for Malcolm X, I knew who he was, but I wasn't too familiar with his ideas. Whenever I heard about him, it was in the *Chicago Tribune*, and they usually had nothing good to say about him. I had heard of Malcolm's mentor, Nation of Islam leader Elijah Muhammad, because Muhammad Ali made him famous. It was not until Ali announced in 1964 that he was a Muslim and had joined the Nation of Islam that a lot of people began to pay attention to the organization. But my religious background was Pentecostal Christianity, which taught that Jesus of Nazareth was the Son of God, while the Nation of Islam taught that God had no son. So I was not enticed by their ideas.

Furthermore, by the time Dr. King arrived in Chicago, Malcolm X had been dead for about a year. If anything, it was the black gangs in Chicago that were getting most of the coverage from the mainstream press whenever attention was focused on the black community; El Rukn and the Blackstone Rangers were the most notorious gangs of the day. The newly formed Black Panther Party was also getting its share of the headlines. In fact, within a year or so, particularly after the dastardly murders of Panthers Mark Clark and Fred Hampton by the Cook County State's Attorney's special police unit, the Panthers would be the main topic of discussion. But I had no more intention of hooking up with them than I had of joining Malcolm X or Dr. King.

I guess if you had to characterize my politics, it would have been like most black Chicagoans, who placed a lot of their faith and trust in William Dawson, a black Democratic congressman who represented the South Side of Chicago. By 1966, Dawson was in his late seventies and near the end of his long tenure in Congress, a tenure that began in 1943. He was revered by most black voters, and I recall Dad talking about the election in 1958, when he ran against another celebrated African American leader: Dr. T. R. M. Howard. After working to find witnesses for Bobo's trial, Dr. Howard had become such a forceful fighter for civil rights in Mississippi that a bounty was put on his head. With his life constantly in danger, he finally fled the South and arrived in Chicago, where as a Republican he unsuccessfully challenged Dawson. I'm not sure whom Dad voted for, since he had great respect and admiration for both politicians. My father never expressed his feelings one way or another about Dr. King and Malcolm X, but I think I got a lot of my fight-back attitude from him.

By this time, Dad was well up in years. During the last years of his life, he lived about a block or so from me. But toward the end, we had to put him in a rest home where there was an attendant to care for him. The last night I visited him, I could tell that he didn't have much longer to live. You could tell by how labored his breathing had become, and you could see it in his eyes. He died in 1977 at the age of eighty-four.

For long periods of time I never discussed, nor was I asked, what had happened to Bobo. I deferred mostly to Mamie, because she had lost her only child, her most precious possession. The only times that I talked about it were at her request. Once she asked me to do an interview with Rich Samuels, a TV reporter out of Chicago. Another time she asked me to speak with a black writer, Dr. Clenora Hudson-Weems.

Mostly it was Mamie talking to the press about her son's murder. She could not bring herself to believe that Bobo would purposely whistle at a white woman after she had warned him of the ways and dangers of the South. So when she gave her take on what had happened at Bryant's store, she didn't say that Bobo didn't whistle, but she offered her own explanation for why he'd made the sound. She said because of his stuttering problem, she had taught him to whistle when he had a problem pronouncing a word. Mamie said that Bobo was trying to ask for bubblegum and began to stutter, so he whistled to get the word out. When people ask me about her version and mine, I tell them first that Mamie was not at the store and second that the whistle happened outside of the store, not while Bobo was buying bubblegum. I tell them that is the love of a mother talking.

During the mid-1980s, Mamie asked my nephew Curtis to give an interview to Henry Hampton, producer of *Eyes on the Prize*, the PBS documentary series about the civil rights movement. Curtis was asked to give his version of what happened at Bryant's store. The problem was, while Curtis was in our home when Bobo was kidnapped, he was not with us at the store the Wednesday before. But he told the filmmakers that we had dared Bobo to go into the store and hit on Carolyn Bryant. He did not mention Bobo's whistle.

Why the late Henry Hampton and the folks at *Eyes on the Prize* didn't come to me or Wheeler, the primary witnesses, is beyond me. Maybe someone was uncomfortable with the idea that Bobo had whistled at Mrs. Bryant. I don't mean to disparage the series, which for the most part is very instructive and uplifting, but I would have told them what really happened at the store. This I know: he did whistle, and we didn't dare Bobo to hit on Mrs. Bryant. If what Curtis said was true, I would confess to the world that it was our fault that Bobo was killed.

We didn't know about what Curtis had said until the series was shown on television. I called Wheeler to see if he had seen the show; he said he had, and we agreed that it had the story all wrong. Even Curtis's brothers and sisters thought he had been an eyewitness. When they found out the truth, they were shocked. When confronted about this, Curtis recanted and said that he was only repeating what he had heard. Unfortunately, Curtis's version is on display at the National Civil Rights Museum in Memphis, Tennessee.

Then one day in the mid-1990s, I was over at Mamie's house and reporter George Curry was there, doing a story for the African American newsmagazine *Emerge*. He asked me some questions about my brother Maurice—he had some erroneous information that Maurice had told Roy Bryant where we lived in exchange for fifty cents of store credit. At that point I became furious. Maurice had been picking cotton Thursday and Friday, and he never did any such thing. Not to mention that Maurice was one of the first to run after Bobo whistled at Mrs. Bryant—but just days later he would put Bobo's life at risk for fifty cents? Now that is sickening. From that moment I refused to talk to anyone about the Emmett Till case.

Around this time, on September 1, 1994, Roy Bryant died of cancer. The same disease had killed his half brother J. W. Milam on December 31, 1980. The news of Bryant's

Bryant's grocery store in 2002.

death didn't bring us any closure—both killers had died without being brought to justice. How sad! I wonder what they will say to the Eternal Judge.

Then, ten years after *Eyes on the Prize*, filmmaker Keith Beauchamp contacted me and wanted to know if I would cooperate in a documentary he was making, seeking to tell Bobo's story. Keith had gotten in touch with me through my sister Hallie, Wheeler's mother, and he then sent me a script he was working on about the case. At first, I was wary about cooperating with him. I was very distrustful of writers, filmmakers, and the press. I felt that they were only interested in a story and not the truth. But my wife, Annie, convinced me to at least talk to Keith and see what he was trying to do. One day he appeared outside my house and called me on the phone. We let him in and began to work with him on his project.

Working with Keith was a breeze. At first he only wanted me on camera to talk about the abduction and the subsequent trial. But after he discovered how much information I had, he decided to shoot longer scenes with me. It was quite an experience and probably the most extensive interviews I had given up to that point. One of the things it forced me to do was to check my facts and to make sure my memory wasn't playing tricks on me. It had been some years since I had been forced to plow back across the years and turn up soil of memories that I preferred to leave buried. Sometimes people think what they remember is the absolute truth, but I found it necessary to go back over a lot of material I had compiled, knowing I was going to be on camera and what I said would be seen by millions of people. Just combing through all the memorabilia brought back a load of unpleasant memories, but I persevered because I didn't want to add to the heap of lies and myths about the case. It was time to tell it exactly like it was, and I was one of the few who could provide the detailed information Keith was seeking.

As I look back now, I believe that if Keith hadn't been so persistent in getting me to work with him, the Emmett Till case would never have been reopened.

8

Reopening the Case and Exhuming the Body

To be honest with you, when I first heard about the drive to get the Till case reopened, I said to myself, "They must be out of their minds." Mamie and her supporters had turned this objective into a crusade, making appeal after appeal to local law enforcement officials and federal authorities, only to have them all fall on deaf ears. Back in 1955, the federal government had refused to investigate the case, and later we were told that the five-year statute of limitations then in place for filing federal civil rights charges had long since

105

expired. But Keith Beauchamp's documentary, *The Untold Story of Emmett Louis Till*, had done much to get the case reopened, uncovering new evidence and locating eyewitnesses. Keith, Mamie, and activist Alvin Sykes, the president of the Emmett Till Justice Campaign, were confident that they had enough information to get the federal government involved. Eventually, they made a believer out of me.

Mamie died in January 2003, but the breakthrough she had hoped for was finally at hand. First, just one month after Mamie's death, the leadership of the NAACP released a statement in support of our efforts to reopen the case. I was elated; I hadn't forgotten how the NAACP had mistreated my father and Mamie, but this was a new day. We needed all the help we could find in the search for justice.

Twelve months later, the Chicago City Council passed a resolution, introduced by Alderman Ed Smith, demanding that the U.S. attorney general launch an investigation into the case. I was not surprised that Bobo's hometown was the first city to do so. Twenty or thirty years ago, people would have said, "Emmett Till got what he deserved." But I was convinced that this generation was better.

In March 2004, Keith, Alvin, my wife, and I traveled to Oxford, Mississippi, with hope in our hearts, to meet with a representative of the U.S. attorney for the Northern District of Mississippi. After I told him what had happened that fateful day, he was visibly shaken. He promised us that he would do all he could to get the case reopened.

To our amazement, we also discovered that the current district attorney of Leflore County was a black woman named Joyce Chiles. I read that she had told a reporter that Keith's film had had a tremendous impact on her. She told us that if the federal government supplied her with all the information she needed on those involved in the murder, she would prosecute.

Two months later, the United States Justice Department announced that it would begin reinvestigating the case.

With that announcement, we were optimistic not only that Bobo's case would find some resolution but that other unsolved murder cases of the civil rights era would also be reopened. At the top of the list was to see Carolyn Bryant convicted as an accessory to murder. I believe she is the person who identified Bobo when her husband and brother-in-law led him out of our house to their truck. I wanted to talk to her and give her a chance to apologize. Her husband and brother-in-law had died with Bobo's blood on their hands, and I wanted her to be able to die with clean hands. I also hoped that Bryant and Milam's other accomplices could be brought to light. Willie Reed had seen four white men and two black men on the truck with Bobo—willingly or unwillingly, they all participated in his murder. And the FBI discovered the deathbed confession of Leslie Milam, the brother of J. W. Milam, who confessed his part in the crime.

Throughout those days, months, years of hope, I often thought about Dad and how he would feel about this new interest in the case. He died thinking that we could never get justice. I guess he never could have imagined that the federal government and the state of Mississippi would be interested in getting to the bottom of things and providing even a glimmer of hope. I knew that he would be very proud—and even prouder if some convictions came.

Soon I was besieged by the media. One reporter wanted to know how I felt about the federal government's involvement and whether they would help or hinder the case. I told him they couldn't hinder it, because the murder trial that took place in Mississippi was already a travesty of justice. Long ago we realized that no justice was coming from Mississippi, so we welcomed the federal probe.

The FBI needed information to further their investigation. The agent in charge, Dale Killinger, met with Wheeler, Uncle Crosby's son Crosby Smith Jr., and me at Wheeler's place in Argo. He told us that the state of Mississippi had informed them that they had to prove that the body now buried in Burr Oak Cemetery was in fact Emmett Till. And to do that, they needed to exhume the body and conduct the autopsy that had never been performed in 1955. I remembered the defense's arguments all throughout the trial that the body was not Bobo. I never had any doubts that it was him, and not just because of the ring.

Wheeler, Crosby, and I granted our permission for the body to be exhumed. (Wheeler didn't really have any say-so in the matter; there were only nine people who actually had the power to authorize the exhumation, and six of them were my brothers and sisters.) I became the contact person for the FBI. They told me that DNA samples had to be taken from one of the next of kin for a process called mitochondrial DNA examination. They first focused on one of my sisters, but in the end the FBI selected me to be the donor. They came to my house and took blood samples, and after that, all I could do was to wait for the day of the exhumation.

As I waited, I heard all kinds of wild things from family members, things that would stress out the faint of heart. Questions like: What if there are no remains? What if his body is not in that casket? What if after the autopsy it is found that the remains are not Bobo? I responded with a question of my own: "What if it is him?"

I was also asked if I thought I could trust the medical examiner. A distant cousin was hounding me to hire my own expert as an onlooker to make sure that the autopsy was performed properly. I refused to even consider her request, letting her know that I had complete confidence in the Cook

County Office of the Medical Examiner and Dale Killinger of the FBI. Her concern defied common sense. The federal government had spent all of this money to investigate the murder of Emmett Till—why would they then misrepresent their findings?

I had no doubts, but I still had to deal with these questions. This would be perhaps my last chance to do something for Bobo. I wasn't about to let the naysayers stop the exhumation. We had come too far to turn back.

On Wednesday, June 1, 2005, the day came for Bobo's body to be exhumed. I remember someone asked me if I was sad. Well, I wasn't sad at all on the exhumation day—I was sad back in 1955. Back then my heart was broken. But on this day I was filled with hope that finally justice would be done.

My wife and I, along with Crosby Smith Jr. and my cousin Ollie Gordon, arrived at the Burr Oak Cemetery in the town of Alsip just before the break of day. No press was allowed on the premises; they waited outside the cemetery gates. A white tent covered the gravesite. My mind raced back to that little church in Mississippi where we had stood beside a grave ready to bury Bobo. I remembered how, just before he was laid in that grave, the sheriff of Leflore County had stopped the proceeding, saying in his Mississippi drawl, "This boy will not be buried in Mississippi, but in Chicago."

I listened to the preacher say a prayer. Then a machine began to tear into the earth. Along with the sound of the backhoe, I could hear helicopters circling above. It was the local news media photographing and videotaping the exhumation. Among the family members there was complete silence. None of us said a word.

Just before noon a concrete vault was hauled from the grave. It was placed on a flatbed truck, which drove off escorted by a convoy of police squad cars. We were told that the body was being taken to the Cook County medical examiner's office, where the autopsy was going to take place.

As the truck drove by the crypt where Mamie was buried, I flashed back to the last time I saw Bobo, when Bryant and Milam forced him out of bed. Bobo seemed to be in a hurry to dress, a sure sign that he was afraid. His face had the look of someone pleading for help. I was mortified with fear and with no means of helping him. Meekly, without saying one word, he left the room with his murderers to face his accuser, Mrs. Bryant.

The officials said they had no idea how long the autopsy would take, but that we would be informed of their findings. I wondered what evidence they would find in the grave or in Bobo's remains after all these years. They could confirm his identity and perhaps determine the cause of death, but other than that I had no idea what they might find. I did know that the last fifty years had brought some revolutionary advances in science and technology, especially what investigators can do with DNA samples and the like. In any event, I hoped digging up Bobo's body wouldn't be just another way of reminding us of his murder and the futility of trying to bring it to closure.

By June 4 the autopsy was completed, and we reburied Bobo's body in a solemn ceremony. But I had heard nothing from the FBI or the medical examiner's office about the results. I was aware, however, that the FBI had assembled quite an impressive amount of material related to the case, which by this time had been going on for more than a year.

Eventually we began to receive information about the autopsy. It put to rest some of the longstanding rumors about Bobo's body. We learned that contrary to many reports, he had not been castrated. Nor were all of his teeth knocked out. There was only one missing tooth on the upper left side of his jaw. The autopsy also dispelled the rumor that Bobo had been tortured by an awl or drill bit to bore holes in his head.

The medical examiner said that the body's dental formation, bone development, and other factors were consistent with that of a fourteen-year-old. There was extensive fracturing of the cranial skeletal remains. The medical examiner concluded that Bobo had died from a gunshot wound to his head and that the manner of death was homicide. We also learned that the body was in excellent condition and there was enough good tissue to conduct a comparative DNA test.

The autopsy results were given to the FBI, who turned them over to the state of Mississippi. From here all the information would go to a grand jury. The FBI was impressed that they had a solid case to charge Carolyn Bryant with manslaughter. But while the FBI was optimistic, there were indications from the media and elsewhere that members of the grand jury and the district attorney's office felt there was not enough evidence to bring charges against Mrs. Bryant. We were left to wonder just how much information was needed.

In 2007, family members were summoned to the Chicago office of the FBI to meet with District Attorney Chiles and go over the grand jury findings. Some of the relatives heard some of the grisly details for the first time, including the fact that Bobo was so badly beaten and his head so swollen that his brain had to be removed before his body was shipped back to Chicago. We also learned the results of the DNA test: the sample taken from the body was a match for the blood samples I had given them—the remains were definitely Bobo's. I was very pleased to hear this, not because I ever questioned it, but because it finally put to rest the lies of Milam and Bryant's supporters.

During the discussion Chiles told us that although Keith had actually found a witness who placed Carolyn Bryant in the truck with her husband and J. W. Milam around 8 P.M. on the night of the kidnapping, she didn't believe that Mrs. Bryant had stayed with them until they showed up at our house at 2 A.M. We were somewhat stunned to hear such a statement coming from the state's prosecutor, and she provided us with no information on how or why she came to that conclusion. But I believe that whoever presented the case to the grand jury shared her inclinations—the grand jury issued no indictments.

This was another terrible setback for the family. As we talked to one another, our sadness only increased. My cousin Airicka Gordon-Taylor was so upset that it was all she could do to hold back her tears. Wheeler said, "I guess they did the best they could. Most of the people are dead anyway." But Bobo's accuser, and the instigator of this whole thing, was still alive. All I could think was that Carolyn Bryant was going to die with the blood of Emmett Till on her hands. She had the chance to get it off, but I knew she would never confess to it now.

My cousin Ollie Gordon, who had taken care of Mamie for many years, was at the meeting and said what most of us felt—that all we wanted was justice for Bobo, but it was not going to come at this time. The probe we thought would bring new answers had come up dry, and there was nothing left to do but pray for another day.

9

Bobo on My Mind

YOGI BERRA SAID, "IT AIN'T OVER TILL IT'S OVER." The grand jury returned no indictments against Carolyn Bryant, but there is always a chance that the case will be revisited. Maybe some young prosecutor with a passion for justice, who doesn't fear losing the case, will give it the support it needs to move forward. Will Emmett Till ever get the justice due him? I don't know. I do know that you can't give up on the quest for it.

I also know the first step in enduring a tragedy such as this one is to have caring people, like my teachers and class-mates, who understand your hurt and accept you with no strings attached. I know it's OK to hurt, but it's not OK to remain stuck in that situation. You must get up and do something. The next step is to forgive those who have harmed you. Believe me, forgiving Milam and the Bryants was not easy, but it was the only way out of this horrific chapter in my life. To those who were involved in Bobo's torture and murder, however, let me make clear that my forgiveness does not exclude you from being prosecuted by the laws of the land.

And even though I've learned how to forgive and to carry on, not a day passes that Bobo doesn't in some way enter my mind.

I think of Bobo whenever I happen to see an article about him in a magazine or newspaper or encounter one of the many books about the murder—so many that I stopped trying to purchase them all. His name has popped up in crossword puzzles, and it was brought to my attention that there is even an online quiz based on Bobo's life. Over the years I've accumulated a lot of documents and memorabilia about the case; now and then I dig them out to refresh my memory, particularly nowadays, when so many people are asking questions. Whenever the media mentions something about Bobo, I receive a slew of phone calls, and letters and photographs arrive regularly. In a way it makes you feel you are part of history, but it's a part no one would ever wish to take on.

There are novels, poems, and plays, all of which attempt to capture some aspect of Bobo's brief life. One play I would like to see is *Blues for Mr. Charlie*, written by James Baldwin as a tribute to Bobo; given his great talent I would love to see his interpretation, though I've been told it's not exactly about Bobo's murder. Bobo's story is also enshrined in song, most notably in "The Death of Emmett Till" by Bob Dylan.

And now rumors are circulating that a feature film is being made based on the incident. Of course, such stories have cropped up several times before without anything ever happening. And knowing how badly Hollywood can mess things up when they try to dramatize a true story—like with the 1988 film *Mississippi Burning*, in which white FBI agents are portrayed as the heroes and blacks are shown only as victims—maybe a movie about Bobo is the last thing we need. Of course, since the story of Bobo's life is in the public domain, we have very little to say about the matter. I imagine, though, that a movie version will one day be made.

I also know how powerful a well-done film can be, from the example of Keith Beauchamp's documentary. There were many years when Bobo was hardly mentioned, but when *The Untold Story of Emmett Louis Till* began screening at various theaters across the country, the public's interest grew considerably. Suddenly, my telephone and doorbell were ringing, and folks were standing outside my house with microphones and cameras. Though I am basically a very shy person, I reluctantly agreed to go on a number of radio and television shows. I wish the attention the documentary provided had been powerful enough to get to the bottom of the murder and bring about more arrests and convictions. But I realize that is impossible. Keith has done as much as he can.

Keith has even gone on to produce and direct four hour-long documentaries that aired on the cable network TV One in the fall of 2008, with the Reverend Al Sharpton as host. The series was called *Murder in Black and White*, and there could not be a more fitting title. Two of the episodes investigated the murders of the Reverend George Wesley Lee and Lamar Smith. I discussed their cases earlier in the book— both men were civil rights activists killed in Mississippi a few months before Bobo's murder because they were too successful in their mission to register more black voters. Now, through Keith's efforts, their martyrdom has been shown to the nation as well.

Keith was also there when I returned to Mississippi in 2005 for the dedication of a highway in Bobo's name. The ceremony took place in Tutwiler, along a stretch of road formerly known as Highway 49E. My family knew it very well, since it was a direct route into Greenwood. The new sign read EMMETT TILL MEMORIAL HIGHWAY, and for a minute I thought that things were at last changing in Mississippi. It upset me to learn a year later, in 2006, that some vandals had defaced the sign with Ku Klux Klan graffiti. The only surprise, however, was that it had taken so long for the race haters to strike.

Nonetheless, I never would have imagined, not even in my wildest dreams, that Bobo's name would one day be immortalized in this way. I've even seen a photo of a marker near the Tallahatchie River, indicating that Bobo was killed about two-and-a-half miles from that location. We had been denied justice, but his name would live long after those who took his life.

Here in Chicago, I see evidence of that legacy whenever I drive on Emmett Till Road or across Emmett Till Memorial Bridge. The road was dedicated back in 1991, with Rosa Parks in attendance. She had Bobo on her mind in 1955 when she decided that she was no longer going to abide by unfair Jim Crow laws and refused to surrender her seat and move to the back of the bus with the other black passengers. "I thought about Emmett Till, and I couldn't go back," Parks often said when asked about her state of mind that day.

Bobo's murder is always cited as one of the major events that ignited the civil rights movement, and both the triumphs and tragedies of that struggle help to keep him in the public's mind. I remember thinking about Bobo when Dr. King led his March on Washington and gave his famous "I have a dream" speech. The date of the rally was August 28, 1963, eight years to the day after Bobo was abducted and murdered.

And I couldn't help but think of him as Hurricane Katrina raged along the Gulf Coast, ripping apart homes and lives. Katrina had become a Category 5 storm and the evacuation of New Orleans had been ordered on August 28, 2005.

But the truth is I don't have to witness a historic event, see a memorial, or read a book to be reminded of Bobo. I think of him every time I hear the sound of a car coming down the road—I remember how I listened that morning in 1955 to the sound of each passing car, hoping that it was Bobo's abductors bringing him back. His life is something I always return to, something that I still live with as I move into my senior years. Even if I become senile, I'm sure Bobo will be on my mind when my mind is no longer my own.

Wheeler is about the only person whom I can really share these memories with, who really understands what happened. Whenever he and I get together, there seems to be a moment or two when we reflect on the past and how our lives were shaped by what happened to Bobo. It may have been Bobo's death that has kept us so very close. Wheeler has committed his life to Christ and is now a pastor in the Church of God in Christ. He has his own church, and I'm a deacon on his board.

It was Wheeler who delivered the eulogy that hot summer day in 2005 when we reburied Bobo's remains. There wasn't a dry eye at the cemetery. Then I asked to say some words. I felt a verse from "Taps" would be the only thing appropriate for Bobo: "Day is done, gone the sun. . . . All is well, safely rest, God is nigh." The image of the headstone is forever etched in my memory: EMMETT L. TILL—IN LOVING MEMORY—JULY 25, 1941–AUGUST 28, 1955.

Epilogue

The Till Bill

JUSTICE FOR BOBO has so far been denied, but all is not lost.

In July 2008, I received a call from Alvin Sykes of the Emmett Till Justice Campaign. He alerted me that members of the U.S. Senate were seeking passage of the Emmett Till Unsolved Civil Rights Crime Bill. The "Till Bill," as it was called, would create a cold case unit at the Justice Department to investigate unsolved civil rights murders that occurred before 1970. The House had already passed the measure in a vote of 422–2, and its supporters in the Senate hoped to follow suit before Congress recessed for the summer. To help their efforts, I was invited to attend a press conference and other meetings by Senators Richard Durbin of Illinois, Patrick Leahy of Vermont, and Christopher Dodd of

Connecticut, scheduled to take place in the office of Senate majority leader Harry Reid of Nevada.

The invitation was similar to the one I had received back in 2005 when the Senate was debating whether to issue a resolution that apologized for failing to prevent the lynching of black Americans and others. I was walking down the Senate halls when a reporter asked me how I felt about the deliberations. I told him that if Congress had passed federal anti-lynching legislation prior to that night in 1955, there's no way men would have come into my house and taken Bobo out and killed him. But since lynching wasn't a federal crime, and they knew the state of Mississippi wasn't going to do anything about it, they could murder him without fear of being held accountable. In the end, I told the press, an apology would be better than nothing. It would at least be a step forward. When the Senate voted in favor of the resolution, that's exactly what it was.

That was more than three years earlier. Now, as my wife and I drove the seven hundred miles from Chicago to the nation's capital, I began to think about how I would respond to the reporters this time. I knew the media was going to be all over me, asking me how I felt about the Till Bill. They would all have a multitude of questions about Bobo, and might even ask me how he would have felt about this new development. What I knew for certain was that the bill would send a clear message to those who continue to violate people's civil rights, and those who did so in the past, letting them know that they wouldn't get away with it. It was hard not to think of J. W. Milam and Roy Bryant, both of whom had escaped justice. Deep in my heart I knew this long drive to Washington had nothing to do with gaining any personal satisfaction—it was for Bobo, whose spirit refused to die, and who was once again on the nation's mind.

When I arrived in Washington, D.C., the press, as expected, was waiting in Senator Reid's office. Senator Durbin welcomed me and asked me what kind of work I did. He seemed pleased when I told him I was a retired pipe fitter. After I was introduced to the other senators, Senator Durbin opened the press conference with a few introductory remarks. He recalled the Emmett Till case with great passion and precision, citing it as one of the worst crimes ever committed in this country. Senator Dodd then explained that the Till Bill had been held up in the Senate for four years, and he insisted it was now time to pass it. I learned that Senator Tom Coburn of Oklahoma was the lone senator blocking the passage of the bill, by using Senate procedures to prevent it from coming to a vote.

I was then asked to share some of my impressions, and I told the press corps about the day nearly fifty-three years ago when Dad and I walked out of the Sumner, Mississippi, courthouse with the feeling that there was no one who could help us find justice. To illustrate some of my feelings, I recalled what had happened to the apostle Paul when the captain of the Roman army ordered him whipped to find out why the people of Jerusalem were in such an uproar against him. As Paul was bound and gagged, he asked of a Roman centurion who stood nearby, "Is it lawful for you to scourge a man who is a Roman and uncondemned?" When the captain heard of this, Paul's beating was halted. My point was that if we as a nation are to achieve the greatness of the Roman Empire, we must be just as diligent about protecting the rights of the least of our citizens as the Romans were. A citizen's rights must not be left up to the states; the federal government must send a message to the ruling classes, both in the South and elsewhere, that if they don't do right by their citizens, then the federal government has the power to enforce those citizens' rights.

I left the press conference and Capitol Hill with a feeling of extreme optimism that the Till Bill would finally be passed. But the bill's supporters needed 60 votes to overcome Senator Coburn's procedural maneuver, and the final tally was 52–40 in favor. Once again, we'd run into a brick wall. The long drive to Washington, D.C., had not been fruitful. I was much disappointed, to say the least, but the seed of recognition for Bobo was planted.

With a few mementos and lots of recent memories, Annie and I headed back to Chicago. We had seen a lot, heard a lot, and we felt that if things hadn't been completely accomplished, at least they were on the right track. One of the best lessons I've learned over the years is that you have to be patient. Things don't always come when you want them, but if you're patient, with prayer and confidence, things will be all right. I felt that eventually the Till Bill would become law.

And on September 24, 2008, I got a call from Senator Harry Reid informing me that the Till Bill had finally passed. Next the bill would be sent to President George W. Bush for him to sign. Right away I thought about Alvin Sykes—he had been the primary force behind the bill, never giving up and making sure the congressional leaders saw the importance of supporting Bobo's legacy. I extend all my good wishes to him for his tireless effort on behalf of Bobo.

I was overjoyed to read that the U.S. Senate had passed the bill unanimously. I was also happy to learn that the bill would allocate ten million dollars a year toward the Justice Department's cold case investigations. This is great news for Keith and other researchers and filmmakers who have devoted so much of their own time and expense toward pursuing these cases. Perhaps even more fortunate are the friends and relatives of those who were victimized by Klan members and other racists during the civil rights era. I am very hopeful that the bill will open new avenues in these loved ones' search for justice and possibly lead to the conviction of some of those responsible. The people who participated in these terrible crimes can no longer rest comfortably.

The president signed the Emmett Till Unsolved Civil Rights Crime Act into law on October 7, 2008. Of all the memorials, monuments, and other commemorations of Bobo's life, nothing pleases me more than to have this bill in tribute to his very brief stay among us, a short life in which he was made a martyr long before he had a chance to live up to his potential. In some respects it's all right that he was just an ordinary boy, because his case has brought about extraordinary possibilities for others whose lives ended tragically. I am sure Bobo would be proud to have this honor. And as his cousin I am immensely grateful that in so many ways he will never be forgotten.

Appendix

Lies, Myths, and Distortions

As I've MENTIONED, a great number of books and articles have been written about the Emmett Till case. Many of them just recount the same information, and they often contain the same lies, myths, and distortions. It's very easy to be a lazy researcher and simply repeat what others have said, but this is a particularly careless practice when you could instead call on eyewitnesses to provide the truth.

On several occasions I've felt compelled to correct some erroneous report or another about the circumstances of Bobo's murder. I imagine this is something a victim's relatives have to live with—even more so when the murder is widely known and becomes the source of much controversy or discussion. I often think about the deaths of Dr. King, Malcolm X, and especially Medgar Evers—whose roots in Mississippi are similar to mine—and how their loved ones had to share their feelings with the world and dispel all the inaccuracies that surround these historical figures.

Keeping Bobo's memory alive and free of misinformation hasn't been an easy task. That's one of the main reasons I decided to take the time and put down my own impressions. I wanted to set the record straight, even if it sometimes meant stepping on the toes of some cherished icons and loved ones.

Among the many inaccuracies that have accumulated over the years, the one that disturbs me most is one of the most often repeated. According to the story, when Dad pointed out J. W. Milam while on the witness stand, he said "Thar he" in broken English. Dad's English was not broken; in fact, he was very careful about his pronunciation and his use of language. As a preacher, he was used to speaking in public, so for anyone to suggest that he spoke so poorly is crazy.

At first I didn't know how this story got started. But then I saw an interview with the late reporter James Hicks, who covered the trial for the *Washington Afro-American* and then became the editor of the *New York Amsterdam News*. When interviewed in his later years for documentaries like *Eyes on the Prize*, Mr. Hicks claimed to have heard my father say "Thar he." But according to Mr. Hicks's own account in the September 24, 1955, issue of the *Afro-American*, Dad said no such thing: "With his thin body racked with emotions, but his face a deadly calm, the Rev. Mr. Wright arose, pointed a bony finger at a white man and declared: 'There he is.'"

Other reports from the time, including the account printed in the September 21, 1955, issue of the *Clarksdale Press Register*, agree with this version of events. So does the official trial transcript, of which I have a copy in my possession. In the following excerpt, Dad is being questioned by District Attorney Chatham, who is trying to establish the identity of the men who kidnapped Bobo:

Q Do you know Mr. Bryant?

A I just know him since he came up here. I couldn't see him that night so well, only with that flashlight there, and I could see that it was this other man, Mr. Milam. But I know Mr. Milam.

Q You know Mr. Milam, do you?

A I sure do.

Q And then what did you do?

A I got up and opened the door.

Q And what did you do when you opened the door?

A   Well, Mr. Milam was standing there at the door
     with a pistol in his right hand and he had a flash-
     light in his left hand.
Q   Now stop there a minute, Uncle Mose. I want
     you to point out Mr. Milam if you see him here.
A   There he is (pointing).

The reports at the time did get it right, but I guess eventually Mr. Hicks decided it would be more dramatic for my
father to sound like a country bumpkin.

James Hicks is also the source of another inaccurate
story, concerning Dad's so-called escape from Mississippi
after the trial was over. According to papers that Mr. Hicks
donated to Washington University in St. Louis, Missouri,
Mr. Hicks and Medgar Evers supposedly hid Dad in a coffin
and took him secretly to Memphis, where he caught a train
to Chicago. (Medgar Evers was never a party to this lie.)
When I am asked about this alleged incident, I answer the
question with a question: What about Mose Wright's three
sons? How did they escape?

Mr. Hicks was, for the most part, a very good journalist,
but those who rely on his coverage of the trial may be mis-
guided, so I feel it's very important to clear up some of his
inaccuracies. Dad didn't say "Thar he," and at no time was he
hidden in a casket for fear of the white man.

Other misconceptions often come up when I'm out speaking to young people at various schools in the Chicago area. The question they ask most frequently is, Why did Bobo whistle? I tell them that he whistled because he wanted to make us laugh.

The students also ask about the story that Bobo had bragged to us about his white girlfriends, showing us the pictures of them in his wallet. I tell them that if he had pictures of any white girlfriends, he never showed them to us. Besides, Bobo went to an all-black school in Chicago. Where would he get a picture of a white girl? These pictures never existed. Those of us who were there have never claimed otherwise—someone just made the story up.

That person was William Bradford Huie. Huie was a writer (he died of a heart attack in 1986 at seventy-six years of age) who made his reputation on expose books. In January 1956 he wrote an article in *Look* magazine titled "The Shocking Story of Approved Killing in Mississippi," one of the most well-known accounts of Bobo's murder. Press releases about Huie often emphasized that he was "in the truth business," but if the truth was his business when he wrote that article, he should have been bankrupt. Most of it was lies and his imagination working overtime.

Huie fabricated the entire conversation he said took place outside of Bryant's store. The way Huie lays it out in his story, it's as though somebody actually told him what happened. But since none of us ever spoke to him—I've talked this over with all the others who were there—he had to have made it up. Not only did we not see any pictures of white girls in his wallet, but we didn't dare him to go in the store and sweet-talk Mrs. Bryant either. Huie also said there were eight of us in the group, including a girl, which is not true. There were six of us, and no girl, as I've explained in this book.

Most of Huie's article was based on the confessions of Roy Bryant and J. W. Milam. Since the jury had found them not guilty, they couldn't be tried again even if they confessed, and Huie apparently paid them four thousand dollars to get them to talk. By then, they probably needed the money, since the stores they had once owned were closed—right after the verdict, blacks in the county stopped going to them. And from what I was told, they had trouble even hiring anybody to work for them, blacks or whites. So that four thousand dollars must have looked pretty good to them. They were ready to say anything to get it, even admitting the truth that they had killed Bobo—and telling a bunch of lies about everything else.

Huie presented the killers' story as the truth, even though there was no way he could verify or challenge what they told him. Because they had agreed to confess to the crime, folks believed that everything else they said was accurate. But while Bobo had been fearful and silent when Bryant and Milam led him away, they claimed that they "were never able to scare him"—that he even talked back as they were beating him. It's hard for me to believe that Bobo said all the things they told Huie; I think claiming that Bobo kept defying them and saying all kinds of ridiculous things was their way of justifying beating him and then killing him.

There is also not a bit of truth in the part of Huie's article that relies on what Carolyn Bryant told him. All she did was retell the story she had testified to during the trial. Again let me state that Bobo was alone in the store for less than a minute, separated from Mrs. Bryant by a counter—he wouldn't have had the opportunity to grab her and ask for a date, as she again claimed.

Even the smaller details of Huie's account were wrong. He contended that Juanita Milam, J.W.'s wife, was in the living quarters in back of the store when we were there. But that was not true; Keith got to the bottom of this lie in his documentary. Huie also wrote that the Bryants sold "snuff-and-fatback" to blacks on credit. No blacks were ever given any credit in the store. In fact, once I was there with a friend who won some money on the slot machine they had in the store, and they refused to pay him. No, they didn't extend any credit to us, and when we had something coming, we couldn't get that.

In the end Huie got his story, with only one truth we can rely on: Bryant and Milam did kill Bobo. Huie got a lot of mileage out of this article, and it definitely enhanced his reputation and earning power, but I'm among those who feel that he was just a "checkbook journalist" who paid for his stories, and we can only speculate about how many of his other efforts were less than credible.

Speaking of stories, there is a play that had a run at the Goodman Theatre in Chicago in May 2008 called *The Ballad of Emmett Till*, by Ifa Bayeza. I saw it and I was completely stunned by one scene in which I'm seen leaving Bobo in Bryant's store alone. Once again a writer has taken certain liberties with the truth. Wheeler and I had actually talked to the playwright a few years before, when she was researching Emmett Till's life. We met at the church where Wheeler is the pastor. I emphasized to her that after I entered the store, I never left Bobo alone there. Then she went right ahead and showed me leaving him alone with Mrs. Bryant. That goes to show you—be careful whom you talk to. Not everyone is a lover of the truth.

There are many more false stories out there. Another one appeared in Clenora Hudson-Weems's 1994 book *Emmett Till: The Sacrificial Lamb of the Civil Rights Movement*. She claimed that my mother refused to give Bobo a train ticket so he could get out of Mississippi after the incident in

Bryant's store. Mom didn't know about the incident—it was Bobo who wanted it to remain a secret. And finally, there's the 1995 article in the now-defunct magazine *Emerge* that claimed my brother Maurice had told Roy Bryant how to get to our house in exchange for a fifty-cent store credit. With stories like that, I see why the magazine went under.

In conclusion, here's my advice to aspiring writers, journalists, and future lawyers—or anyone planning on working in the communications field: if you want an accurate account of any story, go to the primary sources. They know what really happened.

Index

*Italicized page numbers
indicate illustrations*

Ali, Muhammad, 97
Argo, Illinois, 85–88, 91–94
Argo Elementary, 86, 91–93
autopsy, 72, 108–113

Baldwin, James, 117
Ballad of Emmett Till, The (play),
    136
Bayeza, Ifa, 136
Beauchamp, Keith, 102–103, 106,
    107, 113, 117–118
Black Panther Party, 97–98
Blackstone Rangers, 97
Blues for Mr. Charlie (play), 117
Bowers, Sam, 10
Bradley, Mamie Till. *See* Till,
    Mamie Elizabeth
bridge dedication, 119
Brown v. Board of Education, 13

Bryant, Carolyn
    as accessory to murder, 107,
        113–114
    grocery store incident, 50–51,
        135
    at murder trial, 71, 77
Bryant, Roy
    abduction of Emmett Till, 56–59
    arrest, 63
    confession and distortions,
        134–135
    death, 101–102
    kidnapping charges, 89
    at murder trial, 69, 79
    other incidents involving, 83
Bryant's grocery store, 49–51, *50*,
    102, 134, 135
bus travel, and segregation, 8, 119
Bush, George W., 127

Carthan, John Nash, 20, 73
Carthen, Wes, 29

CC riders, 18
Chatham, Gerald, 72, 73, 74, 78
Chicago, Illinois
  civil rights movement in, 94–98
  lifestyle in, compared to
    Mississippi, 85–88
  See also Argo, Illinois
Chicago City Council, 106
Chiles, Joyce, 107, 113
Clark, Mark, 98
Clarksdale Press Register, 131
Coburn, Tom, 125, 126
Cole Wright, Annie, 94, 106, 127
Commercial Appeal (newspaper),
  35
confession, deathbed, 107–108
country-circuit preachers, 18
Crawford, John, 54, 63, 72
Crawford, Roosevelt "Sunnyman,"
  54–55
Curry, George, 101

Dahmer, Vernon, 9–10
Daley, Richard J., 65
Dallas (dog), 30, 82
Dark Fear Road, 25–26, 41,
  45–46
Dawson, William, 98
Dearborn Glass, 94
"Death of Emmett Till, The"
  (Dylan), 117
Diggs, Charles, 73, 74
DNA tests, 109, 113
Dodd, Christopher, 123
Dred Scott, 14
Durbin, Richard, 123, 125
Dylan, Bob, 117

East Money, Mississippi, 25
East Money Church of God in
  Christ, 32, 46, 64–65, 75–76,
  110

education
  in Chicago area, 86, 91–93,
    94
  in South, 3, 13
Eisenhower, Dwight D., 9
El Rukn, 97
Emerge (magazine), 101, 137
Emmett Till case
  accessories to murder, 107,
    113–114
  body exhumation and autopsy,
    108–113
  deathbed confession in,
    107–108
  facts vs. misinformation,
    129–137
  interviews and false
    information, 99–100
  kidnapping charges, 89
  murder trial (*see* Emmett Till
    murder trial)
  reopening of, 105–107
Emmett Till Memorial Highway,
  118–119
Emmett Till murder trial
  courtroom conditions, 70–72,
    73–74
  defense arguments, 72, 77
  depositions, 67–68
  jury selection, 72
  prosecution arguments, 73, 77
  verdict, 78–80
  witnesses, 68–70, 74–77,
    130–132
*Emmett Till: The Sacrificial Lamb
  of the Civil Rights Movement*
  (Hudson-Weems), 136–137
Emmett Till Unsolved Civil
  Rights Crime Act, 123–128
Evers, Medgar, 11, 68, 69, 70, 74,
  132
exhumation, 108–113

Eyes on the Prize (documentary series), 100

FBI (Federal Bureau of Investigation), 107–109, 113
fireworks incident, 42
Fletcher (bully), 46
flu epidemic, 19
Frederick, Grover, 6–7, 26, 81

Gnippe, Irwin Alvin, 92–93
Gordon, Ollie, 110, 114
Gordon-Taylor, Airicka, 114
Great Depression, 16, 34
Greenwood, Mississippi, 3, 4, 53–55
Griffins, Ted, 83

Haley, Mr., 19
Hall, Mamie Smith, 20
Hampton, Fred, 98
Hampton, Henry, 100
Hicks, James, 130–132
highway dedication, 118–119
hog slaughter, 31
hotels, and segregation, 7
Howard, T. R. M., 68, 98
Hudson-Weems, Clenora, 99, 136–137
Huie, William Bradford, 133–136
Hurricane Katrina, 120

Jim Crow laws, 1–4, 7–14, 119
John Russwurm Award, 86
Jones, Buck, 64
Jones, Curtis, 37, 59, 100–101
Jones, Willie Mae Wright, 17, 37, 84
justice system, 4, 9, 14, 79–80, 89–90, 124–128. *See also* Emmett Till murder trial

Katrina, Hurricane, 120
kidnappings
    Emmett Till, 55–57, *56*
    Lindbergh baby, 36–37
Killinger, Dale, 108, 110
King, Martin Luther, Jr., 94–96, 119
Ku Klux Klan, 1, 8–9, 10, 11–12, 118

Larry, Lucinda, 17, 19
Leahy, Patrick, 123
Lee, George Wesley, 11–12, 118
Lee, Huey, 32
Lewis, Clint, 62
Lewis, Gertrude, 62
Lewis, J. T., 64
Lindbergh baby kidnapping, 36–37
loaded pee, 6
Look (magazine), 133
Louis, Joe, 33
lynchings, 9, 10, 25, 63–66, 123–128

Malcolm X, 97–98
Manning, Charles L., 92
Marciano, Rocky, 33
marriage restrictions, 21–22
Mason, Charles Harrison, 19
McShane, Mr., 5
Milam, J. W.
    abduction of Emmett Till, 56–59, 68, 76
    arrest, 63
    confession and distortions, 134–135
    death, 101–102
    kidnapping charges, 89
    at murder trial, 69, 79
Milam, Juanita, 135
Milam, Leslie, 68, 108

military service, 18–19
Mississippi Burning (film), 117
Money, Mississippi, 42, 49–51,
    83–84. *See also* East Money,
    Mississippi
Moody, Rayfield, 73
Muhammad, Elijah, 97
Mullin, Hawkjaw, 36
Murder in Black and White
    (television series), 118
murders, 4, 9, 10, 25, 63–66,
    123–128
music, 34

NAACP (National Association
    for the Advancement of
    Colored People)
    and case reopening, 106
    speaking tours, 86, 87
    Till murder trial involvement,
        66, 68
    See also Evers, Medgar
Nation of Islam, 97
National Civil Rights Museum, 101
Nolan, Eddie, 35–36

Parker, Elaine, 85
Parker, Elbert, 60
Parker, Hallie Mae Wright. *See*
    Wright Parker, Hallie Mae
Parker, Wheeler, Jr.
    barber shop of, 93
    Bryant's grocery store incident,
        49–53
    and case reopening, 114
    description, *85*
    in Greenwood, 54–55
    memories of, 101, 120
    ministry of, 120
    night of kidnapping, *56*, 57, 59,
        60–61
    visit to Mississippi, 37, 39, 48

Parker, Wheeler, Sr., 5
Parker, William (uncle of Wheeler
    Jr.), 60–61
Parker, William (brother of
    Wheeler Jr.), 93
Parks, Rosa, 119
"passing" for white, 21–22
Paul (apostle), 126
Peterson, Mr., 1–2
Peterson, Tommy, 2–3
Ploszek, Charles, 92

rabbit hunting, 30
radio programs, 9, 33, 34, 54
Reed, Willie, 68, 76–77, 107
Reid, Harry, 124, 127
reverse discrimination, 12–13
Reynolds Metals Company, 94
ring, Emmett Till's, *20*, 42, 68, 73
road dedication, 119
Roberts family, 83
Robeson, Paul, 15
Robinson, Sugar Ray, 33
Roy, Ben, 84
Russwurm, John, 86

Samuels, Rich, 99
Sears catalog, 30, 33
segregation
    in Chicago, 86
    in South, 1–4, 7–9, 70–71, 119
Selective Service Act, 18
sharecropping, 4–7
Sharpton, Al, 118
Shelly, Dr., 83
"Shocking Story of Approved
    Killing in Mississippi, The"
    (Huie), 133–136
Smith, Crosby, 60, 64–65
Smith, Crosby, Jr., 108–109, 110
Smith, Ed, 106
Smith, George, 61, 62, 65, 89

Smith, Lamar, 10–11, 118
Smith, Robert B., II, 72, 73, 76
Smith Hall, Mamie, 20
Smith Wright, Elizabeth. *See*
    Wright, Elizabeth Smith
Spearman, Alma Smith, 20, 65
Stevenson, Adlai, 9
Stratton, William, 65
straw bosses, 2, 59
Strider, H. C., 64, 71, 79
Swango, Curtis, 71, 77
Sykes, Alvin, 106, 123, 127

Tallahatchie River, 49–50, 63, 119
Taney, Roger, 14
Till, Emmett "Bobo"
    abduction, 55–60, 56, 111
    birth, 21
    Bryant's grocery store incident,
        49–52
    description, 32, 32 33, 41 42,
        45, 47
    discovery of body and burial,
        63, 64–65
    exhumation and autopsy, 108–113
    in Greenwood, 54–55
    memorials to, 118–119
    misinformation about, 99–100,
        133, 135, 136–137
    with mother, 21
    nickname, 10, 37
    reburial ceremony, 112, 120–121
    ring of, 20, 42, 68
    visits to Mississippi, 37–39,
        42–49
    whistle, 51–52, 99–100, 133
    See also Emmett Till case;
        Emmett Till murder trial
Till, Louis, 20, 20–21
Till, Mamie Elizabeth (Mamie
    Till Bradley)
    and case reopening, 105, 106

    in Chicago, 85
    death, 106
    early years and family, 20
    interviews on son's murder,
        99–100
    marriage to Louis Till, 20–21
    at murder trial, 73, 76, 78
    NAACP speaking tour, 87
    with son, 21
    son's burial arrangements, 65
Till Bill, 123–128
train travel, and segregation, 8

*Untold Story of Emmett Louis Till,
    The* (documentary), 106, 107,
    117

voting rights, 9–11, 12

Ware, John, 5
Washington Afro-American, 130,
    131
whistle, 51–52, 99–100, 133
White, Hugh, 66
White Citizens' Council, 9
Wilson, Woodrow, 18
Wolf, Mr., 42, 83
Wright, Annie Cole, 94, 106, 127
Wright, Cornelius, 17, 84, 85
Wright, Elizabeth Smith
    in Argo, 85
    description, 23, 28
    early years, 19–22
    East Money home and lifestyle,
        26–27, 30–31, 33–36
    leaving Mississippi, 64, 65, 76
    marriage and children, 21–24
    misinformation about,
        136–137
    nicknames, 23
    night of kidnapping, 58–60
Wright, George Arthur, 22

Wright, "Grandpa Billy," 15,
    16–17
Wright, Jackson, 16, 17
Wright, James, 17, 84, 85
Wright, Leah, 84
Wright, Loretha, 22, 28, 32, 37
Wright, Lucinda Larry, 17, 19
Wright, Maurice
    Bryant's grocery store incident,
        49–53
    Carthen confrontation, 29–30
    at East Money home, 26
    and fireworks incident, 42
    in Greenwood, 54–55
    hats and, 32
    misinformation about, 101, 137
    night of kidnapping, 57, 59, 61
    siblings and family, 22–23
    at trial, 70
    watermelon raid, 48
Wright, Moses, Jr., 22
Wright, Moses, Sr.
    in Chicago, 86–87
    civil rights and, 98
    confrontations, 29–30
    description, 22, 27–29, 32
    draft resistance, 18–19
    early years, 15, 16–17
    East Money home and lifestyle,
        26–27, 30–31, 33–36, 43–44
    education and, 31–32
    later years and death, 99

leaving Mississippi, 81–82
NAACP speaking tour, 86
nicknames, 23
as preacher, 18, 19, 32
sharecropping experiences, 4–7
Till kidnapping, 55, 57–62
as trial witness, 74–76, 130–132
wives and children, 17, 19,
    21–23 (see also specific names
    of wives and children)
Wright, Robert
    Crawford trip and, 54
    East Money home, 26
    night of kidnapping, 56, 59,
        61, 62
    siblings and family, 22–23
    at trial, 62
    watermelon raid, 48
Wright, Simeon, photographs of,
    2, 85, 94
Wright, Thelma, 22, 63
Wright, Will, 16, 82, 84
Wright, Willie Crosby, 22–23, 37
Wright Jones, Willie Mae, 17,
    37, 84
Wright Parker, Hallie Mae
    Beauchamp contact and, 102
    in Chicago, 84, 85
    early memories of segregation, 3
    effect of cousin's death, 63
    siblings and family, 17
    Till funeral, 76